UNDERSTANDING
ISRAEL

by SOL SCHARFSTEIN

KTAV Publishing House, Inc.
Hoboken, N.J.

This book
is lovingly dedicated to
my wife

Edythe

Library of Congress Cataloging-in-Publication Data

Scharfstein, Sol.
    Understanding Israel / by Sol Scharfstein.
       p.   cm.
    Includes index.
    ISBN 0-88125-428-2 : $19.95. -- ISBN 0-88125-448-7 : $14.95
    1. Israel--Juvenile literature. [1. Israel.] I. Title.
DS118.S3175 1994
956.94--dc20   94-5791
                                        CIP
                                        AC

Printed in Hong Kong

KTAV Publishing House, Inc.
900 Jefferson Street, Hoboken, NJ 07030

Table of Contents

Table of Contents

INTRODUCTION

For more than 2,000 years of exile, the Jewish people struggled against all odds to realize the age-old dream of returning to Zion. Generations of Jews in exile prayed and waited hungrily for the return to their homeland. The most important moment in Israel's modern history took place in Tel Aviv on May 14, 1948. David Ben-Gurion, the head of Israel's Provisional Council, read the Declaration of Independence that proclaimed an independent state and homeland for the Jewish people. The dream of the return to Zion (Shivat Zion) had become a miraculous reality.

Today, the State of Israel is a coat of many colors: Sabras, Russians, Ashkenazim, Sephardim, Orientals, and Ethiopian Jews with diverse religious, political, cultural, and historical backgrounds all exist in harmony within the Jewish state. Yet, despite the differences, they all have a common Jewish identity rooted in the 5,000 years of Jewish history.

For Israel, the 1990's has been a period of great upheaval, especially the events touched off by the Israeli-PLO Peace Pact. A hopeful Israel is prepared to enter the twenty-first century with a vision of peace with its neighbors.

I hope that this book will help the reader acquire a sense of the extraordinary accomplishments of this tiny country. Thousands of years ago the prophets envisioned a world of peace among nations and a return to Zion. Their prophecy is on the threshold of fulfillment.

Israel is no longer a helpless, underdeveloped, isolated country. Israel is alive and well, and is the homeland of five million Jews and more to come.

ACKNOWLEDGEMENTS

I wish to express my thanks to Howard Adelman, Yaakov Elman, Robert Milch, and Richard White for their scholarly advice and invaluable comments.

————

A special thank-you to June Schwarze for patiently typing the manuscript and for her very valuable suggestions.

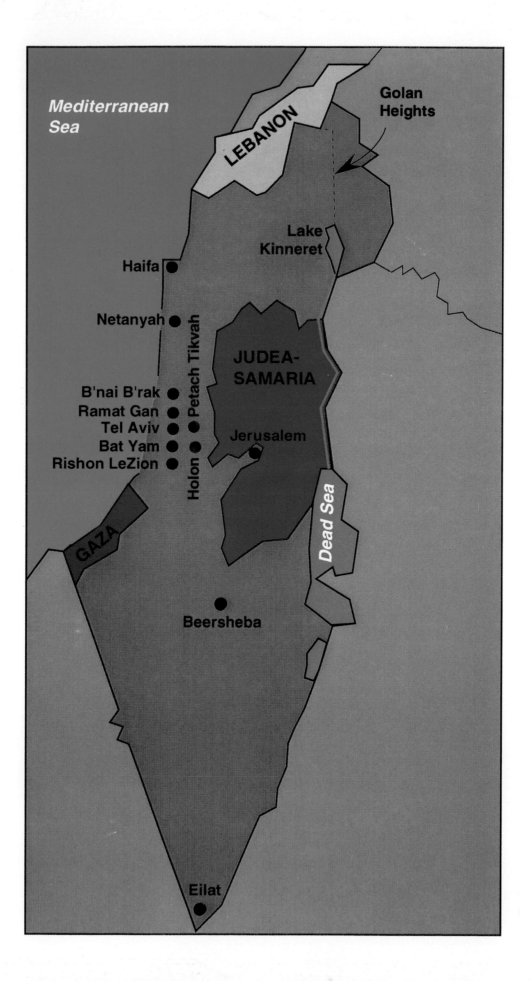

Israel in the World

Israel is located at the junction of three continents: Europe, Asia, and Africa. It is on the eastern shore of the Mediterranean Sea in the region known as the Middle East.

Throughout the course of world history, because of its strategic position between the three continents, the Land of Israel has been the scene of bloody conflicts between warring nations.

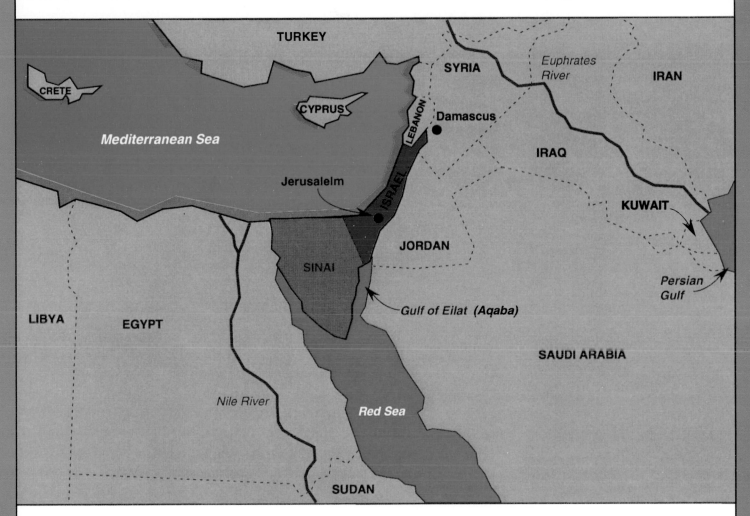

Geography of Israel

The State of Israel is bordered by five Muslim countries: Lebanon to the north, Syria to the northeast, Jordan to the east, Egypt to the southwest, and Saudi Arabia along the Gulf of Eilat.

Israel has a long and narrow shape. It is about 280 miles long and about 85 miles wide at its widest point.

The total area within its boundaries and cease-fire lines is about 11,000 square miles.

The new peace treaty may reduce the Jewish state from 11,000 square miles to 8,000 squares miles.

At its widest point a car can cross Israel from the Mediterranean Sea to the eastern frontier in 90 minutes. The journey from Jerusalem to Tel Aviv is only an hour's drive.

The trip from Metulla, in the far north, to Eilat, the southernmost city, can be made in about seven hours by car.

Jerusalem's altitude is 2,700 feet above sea level. From there to the Dead Sea, which lies 1,300 feet below sea level (the lowest spot in the world), takes less than one hour

Israel is a very small country. It is about as large as the state of Rhode Island in the United States.

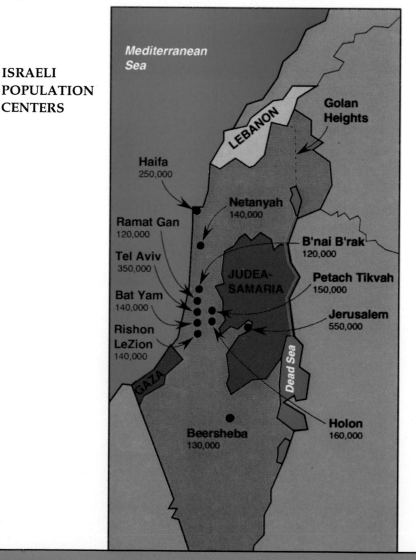

ISRAELI POPULATION CENTERS

Israel's Weather

Israel's wide range of weather results from the amazingly different variety of land forms found in its small area.

These land forms range from burning deserts in the Negev to snow-topped mountains in the Galilee. The Mediterranean coast, with its balmy sea breezes, has warm summers and mild winters, like those of Italy and Spain. Just 40 miles away is the Jordan Valley, which is hot and humid, with temperatures of 110 degrees. This area contains the Dead Sea, the lowest spot on earth.

In general Israel has two seasons, winter and summer. The winters are cold and rainy; in summer the weather is hot and dry.

Winter in Israel is more rainy than cold. Between January and March most of the year's rain pours down, sometimes in torrents that can go on for hours at a time.

Jews all over the world include in their daily prayers a plea for rainfall in Israel during the winter months. God is addressed as the one "who makes the wind blow and the rain fall." Summer in Israel is rainless and very hot. Sometimes, a hot, dust-laden wind blows over the country, lasting for several unpleasant days. This uncomfortable wind is called the *chamsin* in Arabic and the *sharav* in Hebrew. Both words mean the same thing: "burning heat."

During the summer months Israelis go to work early in the morning when the weather is cool. At noon, when the sun is hottest, most people take a break. Some Israelis go home for lunch and a short rest before returning to work. Businesses, stores, banks, and offices shut down for several hours in the middle of the day.

The diversified climate makes Israel an interesting place in which to live. In the winter Israelis can escape the cold, wet climate of Jerusalem by driving only 50 miles to sunbathe beside the Dead Sea.

Neveh Ativ ski resort on the Golan Heights.

As a result of the hot, dry climate, the salty water of the Dead Sea evaporates and forms figures which almost look human. The evil cities of Sodom and Gomorrah were located near the Dead Sea.

According to tradition, it was here that Lot's wife turned into a pillar of salt.

The Regions of Israel

Geographically the Land of Israel may be divided into five distinct parts: the Coastal Plain, the Central Mountains, the Jezreel Valley, the Jordan Rift, and the Negev.

The Coastal Plain lies to the west along the Mediterranean Sea. Here the lush Plain of Sharon with its fertile, well-watered soil links Israel's major cities, Tel Aviv and Haifa. Most of Israel's industry is located here—steel and textile plants, oil refineries, chemical factories—as well as the country's rich vineyards and citrus plantations. Two-thirds of Israel's population lives in the Coastal Plain region.

The Central Mountains extend from the Galilean Mountains of northern Israel through the Judean Mountains of central Israel. Farmers in the valleys of this region grow abundant crops of many varieties of fruits and vegetables as well as wheat, and also raise large numbers of poultry and dairy cattle. Olive groves and newly planted forests cover the rocky slopes of the Galilee. Many Jewish and Arab farm villages coexist peacefully in the Central Mountain region.

The Jezreel Valley, called the Emek ("Valley") in Hebrew, is a flat, fertile region separating the high peaks of the Mountains of Galilee from the lower Mountains of Samaria. The Emek is a region of rich soil, and the proud farmers of its many kibbutzim, moshavim, and privately owned farms raise highly profitable crops of all kinds—wheat, fruits, and vegetables—as well as the dairy cattle and poultry that provide such important elements of the Israeli diet.

The Jordan Rift stretches all the way along Israel's eastern border from the northern to the southern tip of the country. It contains the Huleh Valley, a vast swamp which the early settlers drained, transforming it into rich farmland. The Jordan River flows into the Sea of Galilee (Lake Kinneret) and then down through the very hot Jordan valley, finally ending up in the Dead Sea. The Aravah Valley lies between the Dead Sea and the Gulf of Eilat to the south.

The Negev, the biggest of the five regions of Israel, has the smallest number of people. Until very recently, this large triangle on Israel's south was barren wilderness, a hot, dry desert where no one but roving Bedouin tribes chose to make their home. But the ingenuity and labors of Israel's scientists have paid off. The Negev has begun to bloom. Water piped in from the Jordan River irrigates the desert soil, and crops of vegetables and flowers are flourishing. In addition, the Dead Sea provides important minerals for export and for domestic industries.

The ancient city of Beersheba in the Negev is now a modern town with a population of more than 150,000 Israelis. This bustling city has a world-class hospital and is home to Ben-Gurion University.

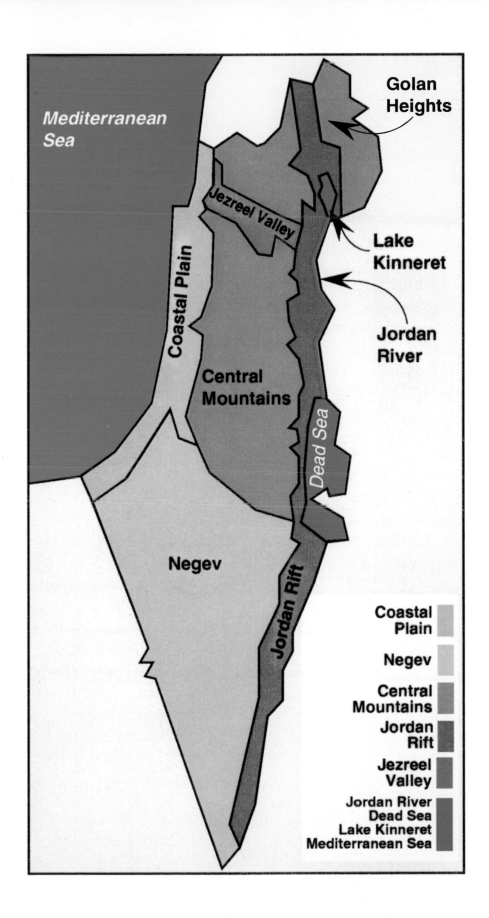

The Environment

Israel's geographical position at the junction of three continents, Europe, Asia, and Africa, has blessed it with a wealth of flora (plants) and fauna (animals). At one time, the Torah tells us, Israel was home to a huge variety of animals, birds, snakes, and fish. Its hills were covered with towering forests and its valleys were carpeted with seas of blooming flowers.

Ancient Israel was a Garden of Eden, with pure air to breathe, clean water to drink, fertile soil for crops, and grassy slopes for flocks of sheep and goats.

During the 3,000 years of Israel's turbulent history, conquering armies and destructive man have damaged and destroyed much of Israel's beautiful natural environment.

Modern Israel is very much concerned about the preservation of the environment. Two organizations, the Society for the Preservation of Nature in Israel (SPNI) and the Jewish National Fund (JNF), are battling to improve and preserve Israel's natural resources.

The SPNI has set up, with government help, some 300 protected nature preserves. It helps conserve the natural landscapes, protect animal, plant, and bird life, and preserve air and water quality. In addition it provides guides for hikers and issues publications to alert the Israeli public about the value of animal and plant life and air and water quality.

The JNF, founded in 1901 by the World Zionist Organization, is also heavily involved in upgrading Israel's natural environment and farmland. During the decades of the resettlement of Israel, the JNF played a key role. With the support of Jews throughout the world who collected coins in their "Blue Boxes," the JNF purchased land that laid the foundation for the Jewish state. The land purchases were the sites for the first kibbutzim and industries.

Under Turkish rule and during the British Mandate, land claims were invalid if the land was not put to use. To establish its claim to the land, the JNF began planting trees.

After purchasing the land, the JNF drained the swamps, planted forests, and made the land arable for agriculture. JNF's goal was to restore life to the land and ensure Israel's future. Great forests appeared on eroded and neglected land. It was the JNF that drained the malaria-infested swamps in the Jezreel Valley and the Huleh Valley that became two of Israel's most productive farming regions.

In the 90 years since its founding, the JNF has, among its many accomplishments, planted 200,000,000 trees and created hundreds of parks and picnic areas. In 1964, the JNF of America inaugurated the John F. Kennedy Memorial and Peace Forest.

To improve the quality of life, the JNF has expanded its activities into water conservation and soil drainage. It has constructed dams to prevent flooding and water reservoirs in the Negev and the Beit Shan Valley.

As Israel's communities grow, SPNI and the JNF continue their efforts to preserve Israel's environment for future generations.

Tu Bishvat is tree-planting time in Israel. These Israeli schoolchildren are planting saplings which will grow into trees for shade and for beauty.

In ancient Israel, parents would plant a tree when a child was born. When two young people married, branches were cut from their trees. These branches were used to support their chuppah—the canopy under which the wedding ceremony took place.

Israeli stamp commemorating the establishment of the Keren Kayemeth Le'Yisrael (Jewish National Fund).

The ibex is a protected species on several of Israel's nature preserves.

The Torah knew the importance of trees. Jews were warned not to destroy trees even during a war. "You may eat of them, but you must not cut them down."

Jews have a special holiday to honor the trees. This special day is called Rosh Hashanah La-ilanot—New Year of the Trees.

The holiday of trees is on Tu Bishvat. The word "Tu" is made up of two Hebrew letters, Tet and Vav. Tet has a numeral value of 9, and Vav has a value of 6. Added together they equal 15. The holiday of Tu Bishvat is on the fifteenth day of the month of Shevat.

The land for the first settlements in Palestine was purchased by Keren Kayemeth Le'Yisrael (Jewish National Fund). It was established in 1901 as the land-purchasing agency of the Zionist movement.

The Jewish National Fund depended on small sums of money collected from Jews throughout the world. The small blue-and-white Jewish National Fund box found a place in millions of Jewish homes.

Jerusalem, the Capital of Israel

Jerusalem is the most special city in the world for Jews, for it is the capital of their homeland, Israel.

In this holy city the prophets and kings of ancient Israel preached and ruled. It was the site of the Temple of King Solomon.

When the Jews returned from the Babylonian exile, they rebuilt their beloved Temple in Jerusalem on the same spot where the First Temple had stood in all its glory. The Romans conquered Jerusalem in 70 C.E. and burned the Second Temple to the ground. All that remained was the fire-charred Western Wall.

In 1948, Jordanian troops captured the ancient section of Jerusalem where the Western Wall stood. The United Nations split up the city of Jerusalem into two parts, and it remained divided for 19 years. Arabs controlled the Old City, and the New City was under Jewish control.

An agreement was signed with the Jordanians allowing Jews into the Old City to worship at the holy places, but the Jordanians did not live up to their promise and refused to allow any Jews into the Old City.

The Jordanians looted and destroyed the historic synagogues and yeshivot in the Old City. They bulldozed ancient graves in the Jewish cemetery on the Mount of Olives.

When the Six-Day War broke out in 1967, Israel promised King Hussein of Jordan that if he kept out of the fight no harm would come to his country. But Hussein was sure that Israel would be defeated, and he began bombing the Jewish part of the city.

Israel counterattacked and after a long battle won back the Old City. Jerusalem once again was a united city.

Steel-helmeted soldiers leaned on the ancient stones of the Western Wall and wept and prayed. A week after the war ended, on Shavuot, 200,000 Jews worshipped at the Western Wall. Their joy at the return of the Jewish people to their sacred city expressed itself in prayer and song.

The date was the 28th day of the Hebrew month of Iyar. Each year on this date Jews celebrate Yom Yerushalayim—Jerusalem Day.

Israelis rejoice at the reuniting of the Holy City and at the same time sadly mourn the brave soldiers who fell in battle.

The Citadel of David stands on the site over which Herod the Great built his palace in the first century B.C.E. At the time of the Jewish revolt against Rome the Citadel of David was one of the main fortifications guarding Jerusalem.
The Byzantine conquerors mistakenly thought that this was David's palace. When the Crusaders invaded Palestine they used the Citadel as a residence and when they were defeated, Saladin used it as his headquarters. The tall minaret was added in 1655.

This ancient block of stone was a part of the wall of a building in the Temple compound in Jerusalem. The Hebrew inscription reads, "To the place of trumpeting."

In Temple days a priest would stand on a roof and announce by shofar blasts the approach and end of Shabbat.

This inscription illustrates one of the ancient modes of communication between the priests in the Temple and the people of Jerusalem.

Today, in some heavily populated Orthodox communities, a siren is used to announce Shabbat.

The interior of the Yohanan ben Zakkai Sephardic Synagogue in the Jewish Quarter of Old Jerusalem. It is one of the oldest synagogues in Meah Shearim. In 1948 the synagogue was destroyed by the Arab Legion. It was rebuilt in 1972.

The Romans conquered Jerusalem in 70 C.E. and burned the Temple to the ground. All that remained was the Western Wall, which became a sacred place where Jews worshipped and prayed for the independence of Israel. All through the centuries of exile Jews worshipped at the Western Wall. The Wall is considered so holy that it has become a custom for Jews to write their prayers on pieces of paper and wedge them into the cracks between the stones.

Tel Aviv–Yaffo

In 1907 Tel Aviv was nothing more than a series of sand dunes along the Mediterranean coast. Today, it is the largest and most modern city in Israel. Tel Aviv is home to about 350,000 Jews.

Tel Aviv–Yaffo is a combination of two cities. Yaffo (Jaffa) was one of Israel's oldest cities, and Tel Aviv was one of the newest. In 1929 these two cities merged.

Tel Aviv–Yaffo, like most modern cities, is a study in contrasts. Some parts of the city are decaying slums where people live in crowded, run-down apartments. Other parts are attractive, well-kept residential areas with elegant houses and beautiful parks.

Most of Israel's big business firms and banks have their administrative offices in Tel Aviv, as do Israel's book and newspaper publishers. Almost half of Israel's factories are located in or close to Tel Aviv.

There is a fun aspect to Tel Aviv–Yaffo. This sparkling city is known as Israel's playground. There are spacious parks, discotheques, large department stores, theaters, operas, libraries, and a large zoo. In addition, Tel Aviv is home to one of the world's finest orchestras, the Israel Philharmonic. Along the coast a whole chain of hotels have been built, most of them with their own beach and entertainment centers.

The two main thoroughfares of Tel Aviv are Dizengoff Street and Allenby Street. Dizengoff Street is named after the city's first mayor, Meir Dizengoff. Allenby Street is named after the British general, Sir Edmund Allenby, who captured Israel (then called Palestine) from Turkey in 1917.

In the evenings Tel Aviv's busy cultural centers attract Israelis and tourists who love opera, theater, and cinema. Tel Aviv–Yaffo, like most large cities, is surrounded by a ring of suburbs. These towns, such as Herzliya, Netanyah, and Bat Yam, are the bedroom communities of Tel Aviv. In the mornings and in the evenings, as in all major cities, there are traffic jams with commuters fighting their way to their jobs and businesses.

Proud Tel Avivniks like to compare their hometown to New York City—the Big Apple. They call Tel Aviv the Big Orange.

Tel Aviv at night. Its sparkling lights illuminate the skyline.

In 1909 Tel Aviv was nothing more than a series of sand dunes. This rare old photo shows the allocation of plots of land to the first residents of Tel Aviv.

Aerial view of the seashore of Tel Aviv.

A falafel stand in Tel Aviv. Falafel is a Yemenite delicacy made from chickpeas. The mashed peas are fried and sandwiched into the center of a pita. The falafel is then covered with a variety of sauces and salads, some of which are hot enough to burn your throat. Falafel is to Israel what pizza is to Italy.

The Shalom Tower is the tallest building in Tel Aviv. The top floor has an observatory.

Exterior view of the Mann Auditorium in Tel Aviv. It is the home of the Israel Philharmonic Orchestra. With a seating capacity of 3,000, it is Israel's major concert hall.

Haifa

There is a saying among Israelis that Jerusalem is the soul of their nation, Tel Aviv the heart, and Haifa the muscle.

Haifa is Israel's third-largest city with about 250,000 people. It is located on the Mediterranean, occupying the slopes of Mount Carmel and the low-lying land at its base. Because of the mountain, the city of Haifa is built on three levels, just like a three-layer cake. The first level is the old city and the port area, which pulses with energy. In Haifa's port you can see speedy warships, smelly fishing boats, and huge merchant vessels from all over the world.

Haifa is an important center for heavy industry. Its industrial plants include such factories as Nesher Cement, Vulcan Foundry, Phoenicia Glass, large smoky steel mills, and busy shipyards. The port of Haifa also has an oil zone with refineries and oil storage tanks.

Haifa is home to the world-famous Technion, the Israel Institute of Technology, known as Israel's M.I.T. It deals with the most modern advanced sciences, such as nuclear physics, electronics, all types of engineering, and aerodynamics.

Halfway up the slope is the second layer of the cake. This area is called Hadar Ha-Carmel, "The Beauty of Carmel." Rising from the wooded slopes of the mountain are hundreds of modern apartment buildings, their balconies facing the breezy blue Mediterranean. This residential part of the city is self-contained and has its own shopping and recreational areas.

The third layer, the icing on the cake, is called Har Ha-Carmel, "The Mountain of Carmel." This area is a very popular vacation and health resort. Winding mountain trails and bridle paths offer many opportunities for hiking and horseback riding.

Israel's only subway, the Carmelit, is in the city of Haifa. It connects the lower-level harbor area with the other two layers. The mountain slopes are so steep that cars and buses can only make their way up and down by following winding roads that circle the mountain. By the Carmelit subway it takes nine minutes to go from the port to the top of Har Ha-Carmel. This subway saves the people of Haifa many hours of travel.

Haifa's most impressive attraction is the golden-domed Shrine of the Bab. It contains the tomb of the Bab, the founder of the Bahai religion. Haifa is the headquarters of the Bahai.

A view of Haifa Bay from atop the mountain. The Bahai Temple is in the foreground. The blue waters of Haifa Bay glisten in the background.

A view of Haifa from the heights of Har Ha-Carmel. Some say that the name Haifa comes from the two Hebrew words *hof yafeh,* meaning "beautiful coast."

Israeli stamp issued in honor of the Technion in Haifa.

In the early 1900's Haifa was a small sleepy fishing village and Mount Carmel was uninhabited. Its port was marshland and sand dunes lined the coast.

Beersheba

Beersheba is the capital of the Negev, Israel's largest region. The city of Beersheba is even older than Jerusalem. Israel's ancestors Abraham, Sarah, Isaac, Rebecca, Jacob, Rachel, and Leah all lived and traveled in this area.

In World War I the town was captured from the Turks by the British under the command of General Allenby.

During the War of Independence in 1948, the Egyptians occupied Beersheba but were driven out by the Israel Defense Forces.

Today, this tiny, sleepy town has awakened from its long slumber and is now a very modern, busy, bustling city of over 130,000 people. It is home to the Ben-Gurion University of the Negev with thousands of students. This sophisticated seat of learning includes medical and engineering schools. Its scientists and doctors specialize in subjects which can help increase the potential of the Negev. Among the projects are desalinization plants and the cultivation of desert crops.

The Negev is slowly coming to life. Water from the Jordan River and the National Water Carrier is piped into kibbutzim that raise large crops of fruits, vegetables, and flowers which are exported to Europe and the United States.

Beersheba is also known for its Bedouin market. Each Thursday this modern city turns back the clock and reverts to the days of Abraham, Isaac, and Jacob. The Bedouin market opens at 6:00 o'clock in the morning and everything is for sale. Grumbling camels, baaing sheep, cackling chickens—all are for sale side-by-side with second-hand cars, Japanese tele-vision sets, and Levi's jeans. Sacks of fruits, vegetables, and grain are bought and sold over traditional cups of coffee with much good-natured bargaining. The Bedouins are dressed in traditional desert clothing with shiny Rollex watches on their wrists and Walkman radios glued to their ears.

By noon the market is over. The knights of the desert mount their jeeps and trucks and ride off to their black tents in the desert with their radios blaring.

Beersheba is a metropolis with a dual personality: one foot planted in the Bible, the other in the twentieth century.

The Bedouin market in Beersheba.

In 1917 the British Army under the command of General Allenby captured Beersheba from the Turks. This photograph shows the surrender of the city by the Turkish garrison to two British sergeants.

The patriarchs and matriarchs of Israel traveled to and around the ancient city of Beersheba,. The Bible mentions a treaty that Abraham made with Abimelech, a Philistine king. The treaty involved settling a dispute about a well that Abimelech's servants had seized from Abraham. Abraham sealed the treaty by giving the king seven sheep.

Some say that Beersheba means "well of the seven," referring to the seven sheep and the well. As a sign of the treaty, Abraham planted a tamarisk tree at the "well of the seven." Another explanation is given on the opposite page.

Today in Beersheba there is an ancient well near a tamarisk tree, which some say dates from the time of Abraham.

This photo shows a tamarisk tree with Beersheba in the background.

Ben-Gurion University.

The Druze

The Druze are Arabs but not Muslims. They have their own special religion. They believe that Jethro, the father-in-law of Moses, was one of God's prophets. Jethro's tomb near Tiberias is a holy Druze shrine.

Ismail ad-Dazai founded the Druze religion in the eleventh century. They keep their religion secret from outsiders. The Druze forbid intermarriage and do not accept converts.

Although the Druze speak Arabic, they are separate from the Arab community. During the War of Independence the Druze fought in the Israeli army. Today the IDF (Israel Defense Forces) has Druze units that specialize in desert warfare.

The Druze are represented in all phases of Israeli life. Hundreds of Druze young people attend Israeli institutions of higher learning. Druze politicians have been candidates for election to the Knesset.

Israel's Druze populace lives in several villages in the Galilee and on Mount Carmel. After the Six-Day War Israel annexed the Golan Heights, and as a result the Druze villages in that area also became part of Israel.

A Druze desert warfare military unit on parade.

The Bedouins

The Bedouins are the wandering tribesmen of the Middle East. They pitch their goatskin tents wherever they find grass for their sheep, goats, and camels. The Bedouins dress in a long robe called a *thawb*. On their heads they wear a white scarf called a *kaffiyah*. There are 110,000 Bedouins in Israel, and half of them still continue their nomadic desert life.

Bedouins are known all over the world as friendly hosts. They also have another distinction. They are the world's best trackers. As trackers they are serve in the IDF units that patrol Israel's borders.

Thursday is market day in Beersheba, the capital of the Negev. The Bedouins trade their sheep and goats and also sell their produce. Some bring their animals in pick-up trucks, and some come in riding on camels.

The Bedouins are known as the "Lords of the Desert." Bedouin caravans are constantly on the move searching for places to graze their flocks of sheep, goats and camels. The camel is especially suited for desert travel.

As the Negev has become more cultivated, there is less grass for the flocks and for planting. As a result, many Bedouins have established permanent homes and send their children to Israeli schools. Bedouins serve in the Israel Defense Forces.

The Samaritans

The Samaritans were once a fairly sizable religious community. Today only about 600 people still accept the Samaritan faith. Half of them live in the town of Nablus, near Mount Gerizim. The other half live in Holon near Tel Aviv.

In ancient times the Samaritans were often in conflict with the Jews. They acknowledge Moses as a prophet and claim to be descended from Ephraim and Manasseh, the two sons of Joseph. They accept the Torah and the Book of Joshua as holy, but not the rest of the Bible.

Passover is the Samaritans' most important holiday. It is celebrated on top of Mount Gerizim. The Passover feast is

The Torah of the Samaritans is housed in the synagogue in Nablus. It is written in ancient Hebrew and is extremely old.

celebrated just as it was thousands of years ago. A lamb is sacrificed and matzot are baked the ancient way.

The Russians

For about 2,000 years, the Land of Israel was in the hands of foreigners. In 1948 a miracle occurred and the land the Roman conquerors had renamed Palestine once more resumed its rightful name—Israel. To make sure that all Jews would be welcome in the homeland, the Knesset passed the Law of Return. Under this law all Jews, no matter what country they live in, have the right to become Israeli citizens if they come and live in Israel.

The Law of Return helped make the age-old dream of Shivat Zion ("Return to Zion") and Kibbutz G'luyot ("Ingathering of the Exiles") a reality.

The Israeli government has designed two techniques to ease the absorption of new immigrants (olim): direct absorption and absorption centers.

Olim spend their first six months in a residential ulpan where they study Hebrew and learn all about their new country. At the end of six months they are provided with an apartment, preferably near their friends and relatives.

As a result of the collapse of the Soviet Union, more than 450,000 Russians have made aliyah to Israel. Between 1990 and 1994, the huge population explosion of Russian olim has changed the social structure and thinking of the Israelis.

On the streets of Israel one hears almost as much Russian as Hebrew. Russian newspapers, magazines, billboard advertisements, books, plays, and music are very common. The flood of Russian olim has also created many problems for the tiny state. There are shortages of housing and welfare, and hospital costs are zooming through the roof. However, the most pressing problem is the shortage of high-quality professional jobs. The four-letter word "jobs" is casting a very worrisome shadow over Israel's economy.

The good news is that jobs are being created. After 40 years of wandering, Israel's economy seems to be finding its way. The country with the highest proportion of scientists and engineers in the whole world is slowly, but surely, on its way to becoming an economic Samson.

There are now about 50 Israeli high-tech companies on the American Stock Exchange. Jobs are coming, but unfortunately, not fast enough.

With all the problems—no jobs, a new language, the military situation—the Russians keep on coming. Difficult economic conditions in Russia and the other countries that once comprised the Soviet Union have accelerated anti-Semitism, and a desire to return to Judaism has kept the stream of olim coming.

The United States has guaranteed a $10 billion loan. It is not giving the money to Israel. Israel is borrowing the money from private banks which it has to repay. Because the United States guarantees repayment, the government of Israel is charged much less interest.

Jews all over the world also contribute to the resettlement and training of Russian Jewry. Above all, the Israelis have opened their country and their hearts to their Russian brothers and sisters.

The age-old talmudic saying "All Jews are responsible for each other" is the Israeli motto.

Former Prime Minister Yitzchak Shamir addresses the participants in a Bar Mitzvah celebration for 90 immigrant children from the Soviet Union. This celebration was sponsored by the Lubavitch religious movement.

Newly arrived Russian immigrants.

ANATOLE (NATAN) SHARANSKY (1948-)
Scientist, Activist, Refusenik.
Anatole Sharansky is a Jewish computer scientist who helped organize the Jewish refusenik movement in the USSR. In 1973, because of his activities, he was arrested and kept in solitary confinement for 18 months. He was finally placed on trial on the trumped-up charge of espionage. Despite worldwide protests Anatole was sentenced to 13 years of imprisonment.

After 11 years in prison and labor camps, he was released and immediately left for Israel. Anatole Sharansky, activist and refusenik, now leads the fight for the rights and welfare of new Soviet immigrants in Israel.

This chart illustrates the dramatic rise of Russian immigration. The Russian Aliyah has had a positive effect on Israeli life.

SOVIET ALIYAH
(Numbers of Russian immigrants by year since 1986)

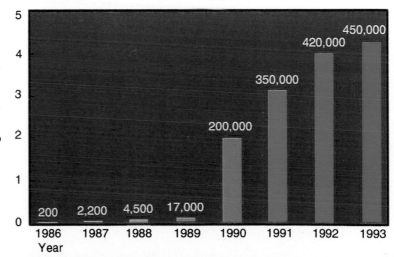

Number of immigrants, in 100,000's

Year	Number
1986	200
1987	2,200
1988	4,500
1989	17,000
1990	200,000
1991	350,000
1992	420,000
1993	450,000

On Wings of Eagles

Yemen (Tayman) is a small country located on the Arabian Peninsula. According to tradition, the Jewish community of Yemen dates back to the time of the destruction of the First Temple in 586 B.C.E.

For many centuries the Jews of Yemen lived in peace with their Arab neighbors and maintained strong religious and communal ties with the Jews of Egypt and Iraq. However, in the twelfth century, Arab persecution forced them to cut their ties to the outside world. They were despised by the Arabs and forced to live in ghettos and even in mountain caves.

Despite their enforced poverty, the Yemenite Jews (Taymanim) remained a hard-working, deeply religious people. They were so poor that there were not enough Bibles for all the children in the schools. Several would have to crowd around each Bible, looking at it from different directions. As a result, Yemenite children learned to read upside down and sideways as well as the usual way.

Jews were barred from participating in the normal economic life of Yemen. However, they were allowed to become silversmiths, since the Islamic religion forbids believers to work in silver and gold. Yemenite Jews became famous for creating unique jewelry and beautifully embroidered clothing.

The struggle for survival in an alien environment led some Yemenite Jews to seek refuge in Israel. A large group emigrated to Israel in 1882 and settled in Jerusalem. Soon afterwards other Taymanim settled in the farming villages of Rehovot, Rishon Le-Zion, and Petach Tikvah.

To the downtrodden Yemenite Jew the establishment of the State of Israel was the beginning of the fulfillment of the biblical prophecy that God would bring the Jews back to Israel "on the wings of eagles."

In 1949 the "eagles" came in the form of giant El-Al planes. More than 50,000 Yemenite Jews were flown to Israel in Operation Magic Carpet.

As each of the "eagles" landed in Israel, the deliriously happy Taymanim kissed the ground and sang psalms of praise.

Adjusting from a medieval way of life to a modern civilization was not easy for the Jews of Yemen. Modern conveniences such as running water, toilets, and automobiles were completely foreign to them.

The Yemenite Jews became a great asset to the State of Israel. They have made a major contribution to Israeli culture. Their artistic skills, their music, and their industriousness have helped make Israel prosperous.

A Yemenite blowing the shofar at the Western Wall.

In the hands of skilled Yemenite craftsmen, gold, silver, and precious stones are transformed into a beautiful Torah crown.

A Passover Seder as conducted by a Yemenite family.

This Yemenite family, brought to Israel during Operation Magic Carpet, was first lodged in a temporary camp called a *maabarah*. After a period of orientation the family was transferred to a farm settlement. The Yemenites have a love for the land and quickly became successful farmers. They mastered modern methods of farming and become an important social and economic asset to the State of Israel.

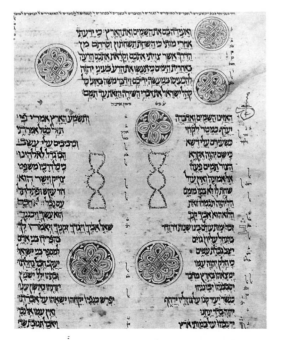

A page from an illuminated Yemenite Five Books of Moses. This manuscript was completed in 1496 C.E. for Ibrahim ibn Yusuf ibn Sa'id ibn Ibrahim al-Israili. The text is a section of the Song of Moses.

The Muslims

Islam is the religion of the Muslims. About 15 percent of Israel's population is made up of Arabs, most of whom are Muslims

Who are the Muslims, and how did they get to Israel?

Muhammad, a trader from the city of Mecca in Arabia, founded the Muslim religion. He claimed that the angel Gabriel had come to him in a dream and said, *"Muhammad rasul-u-l-lah"* ("Muhammad is Allah's prophet").

Muslim teachings are recorded in a sacred book called the Koran. Muslims believe that Abraham, Moses, Elijah, and Jesus were messengers of God. Religious Muslims pray five times a day; they kneel toward Mecca and recite verses from the Koran.

Mecca in Saudi Arabia is the Muslim holy city. Once in their lives, Muslims try to make a pilgrimage to Mecca. There they pray at a shrine called the Kaaba. Muslims believe that the Kaaba was built by Abraham and his son Ishmael. Each year thousands of Muslim pilgrims go to Mecca to pray. This pilgrimage is called a *haj.*

All over Israel the Muslim call to prayer can be heard from the tall towers of the mosques. As they enter the mosque Muslims must remove their shoes and wash before they begin to pray.

Muhammad died in 632 C.E. Today Islam is the second-largest religion in the world.

Jerusalem is the home of the beautiful Mosque of Omar, built on the site of King Solomon's Temple. Inside the mosque is the rock upon which, according to tradition, Abraham offered his son Isaac as a sacrifice. Muslim legend claims that Muhammad ascended into the heavens from this rock.

The majority of Israel's Muslim Arabs live in cities and in farming villages. Arab workers are full-fledged members of the Histadrut, Israel's largest labor union. Muslim Arab citizens have the same rights as Jews, except for serving in the Israel Defense Forces, and are represented in the Knesset by several Arab members.

Arab children receive the same public education as Jewish children, from kindergarten through college.

Israeli Jews and Israeli Arabs hope that a peace treaty will ease the tensions between them.

The golden dome of the Mosque of Omar in Jerusalem is a highly visible landmark. It was built by Caliph Abdul Malik Ibn Marwan in 691 C.E.

An ancient painting showing Muhammad with the leader of a Jewish tribe in Arabia. He condemned the whole tribe to death because they refused to convert to the Muslim religion.

A page from an ancient copy of the Koran. Illuminated copies of the Koran were skillfully handwritten and illustrated in gold and bright colors.

Israeli stamp with minaret.

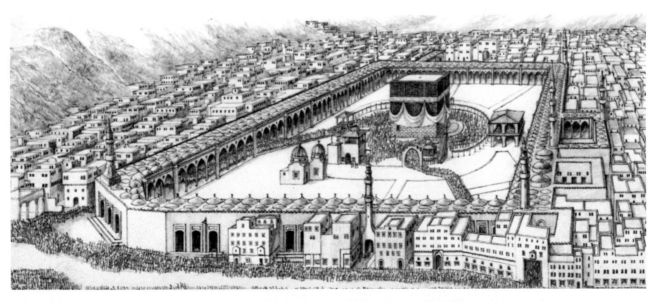

The holy city of Mecca and its mosque. Near the center of the mosque is a small shrine called the Kaaba. Muslims believe that the Kaaba was built by Abraham and Ishmael. Embedded in one wall of the Kaaba is a black stone. Muslims believe the stone was given to Adam by an angel. Each year thousands of Muslim pilgrims come from far away to kiss the sacred black stone.

A Coat of Many Colors

Israel' population is over five million, and is still growing. It is a "coat of many colors" with Jews of varied hues and backgrounds from every continent and clime.

Israel's "coat of many colors" includes Ashkenazim, Sephardim, Edut Ha-Mizrach (Oriental Jews), and Falashas. This diverse population has combined the special skills, talents, and energy of its members to build the most modern state in the Middle East.

Ashkenazim are Jews whose ancestors lived in northern and eastern Europe: Germany, Russia, Poland, and the neighboring countries. These Jews developed the Yiddish language, which is a Germanic dialect written in Hebrew script.

The Ashkenazim first came to Israel in the sixteenth century and settled in the four holy cities of Jerusalem, Hebron, Tiberias, and Safed. Most of the Zionist settlers who built up Palestine during the First and Second Aliyot were Ashkenazim from northern Europe.

Sephardim are Jews whose ancestors lived in Spain (Sepharad) until they were driven out in 1492. Until the twentieth century many of them lived in Turkey and the Balkan countries. Like the Ashkenazim, the Sephardim developed their own special language, called Ladino. This language is a mixture of Spanish, Italian, and Greek, and like Yiddish is written in Hebrew script.

Many Sephardic Jews settled in Palestine after the Spanish Expulsion in 1492. Until the First and Second Aliyot, most of the country's Jewish inhabitants were Sephardim. Some of the oldest families in Israel are descended from Sephardim.

The Edut Ha-Mizrach are Jews from countries such as Egypt, Morocco, Algeria, Tunisia, and Libya. Their language is Arabic. Closely related are Jews from the other Arab countries, such as Iraq and Yemen.

The Falasha, also known as the Beta Israel, are black Jews from Ethiopia. Until modern times they had virtually no contact with the rest of world Jewry. Since the 1960s the entire Jewish community of Ethiopia has immigrated to Israel. The warm welcome they have received has demonstrated to the world that there is no racism in Israel.

In addition to these major groups the population of Israel includes smaller groups of distinct culture and history, such as the Bene Israel from India.

In Israel these many groups are not separated by barriers of space and distance. They live side by side; their children attend the same schools, and their sons and daughters serve in the same army. They all speak the same language, Hebrew, and their children, born in Israel, have one common name: Sabra.

The sabra is the fruit of a cactus bush, prickly and tough on the outside and juicy and soft on the inside. This word has become the nickname for native-born Israelis.

A group of Kurdistan Jews in transit to Israel. Operation Ali Baba, an airlift, brought 120,000 Jews from Iraq to Israel. Operation Ali Baba began in 1951.

Ethiopian immigrants on Israeli air force plane from Addis Ababa to Israel during Operation Solomon.

The thorny sabra plant and its sweet and juicy fruits. Natives Israelis are called sabras because they are thorny on the outside, but friendly, when you get to know them.

IMMIGRATION (Aliyah) FROM ARAB COUNTRIES

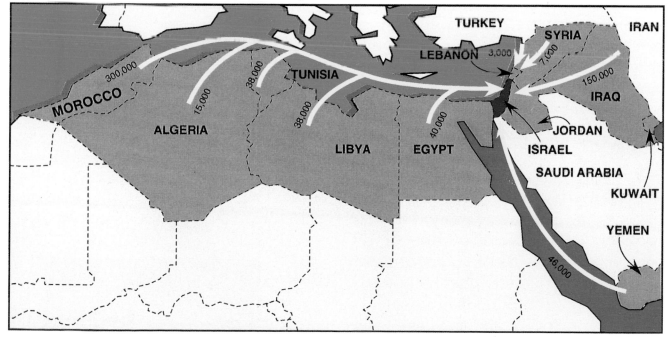

Israeli independence had a tremendous effect on Jewish communities in Arab lands. Most of the Arab countries instituted severe restrictions on their Jewish citizens. The hostile governments deprived them of their properties, their homes and their businesses.

These repressive measures initiated a huge exodus of Jews from the Arab countries to Israel. Most of the Jews arrived penniless, with only the clothes on their backs.

In 1949, Operation Magic Carpet evacuated 50,000 Jews from Yemen.

Symbols of Israel

Every country in the world is different. Each and every country has its own special language, its unique national anthem and emblem, and its own colorful flag.

Israel's population is made up of people from all over the globe, who speak a dizzying variety of languages, eat different foods, dance and sing to their own special music.

With all these differences, there are links which connect all of these people into one solid nation. These links are in language, anthem, flag, and national symbol. Each of these links is rooted in Israel's historical experiences and religious ideals.

Israel's official language is Hebrew. The same 4,000-year-old language our ancestors spoke in Israel long, long ago. Even when Jews were driven out of Israel, they continued to study the Torah and to pray in Hebrew. The ancient language was never forgotten.

In 1881 Eliezer Ben-Yehuda began to revive and modernize the Hebrew language. He compiled a large dictionary with thousands of new words that made it possible to discuss modern ideas and technology in Hebrew. Today, Hebrew is spoken in the beauty parlors of Tel Aviv, the soccer fields of Haifa, and the supermarkets of Israel. The 4,000-year-old language of the Bible is alive on TV, newspapers, rap records, and computer programs.

The Hatikvah is Israel's national anthem. Naphtali Herz Imber composed the anthem in 1878.

The word *hatikvah* means "hope." Throughout the thousands of years of exile, wherever Jews lived, they never lost hope. They always had *hatikvah* that they would someday return to the restored nation of Israel.

In 1948, their hope was finally realized. Israel was reborn. Today, wherever Jews live and work, they sing the Hatikvah with pride.

The Torah describes the flags of the twelve tribes of Israel, but there is no mention of a flag for the nation of Israel.

In 1889 David Wolffsohn designed the flag of Israel that is in use today. He used the blue-and-white stripes of the tallit and added a Magen David (six-pointed star) in the center.

The six-pointed star is known in English as the Star of David. Some people believe that King David had a six-pointed star on his battle shield.

The emblem of Israel tells us a lot about the history and ideals of the Jewish people.

The Temple menorah in the emblem reminds us of the glory of the city of Jerusalem and also of its sad destruction.

The olive branches are symbols of peace. They tell the world that Israel wishes to live in peace with its neighbors.

The blue-and-white flag of Israel

The emblem of the modern State of Israel. The ancient Temple menorah is surrounded by olive branches. Olive branches are symbols of peace.

As long as deep in the heart,
The soul of a Jew yearns,
And towards the East
An eye looks to Zion,
Our hope is not yet lost,
The hope of two thousand years,
To be a free people in our land,
The land of Zion and Jerusalem.

This huge bronze menorah is in the Knesset courtyard in Jerusalem. It was a gift from the people of England to Israel.

ISRAEL – 25 YEARS OF INDEPENDENCE

An Israeli stamp showing part of the Declaration of Independence.

Eretz Yisrael (the Land of Israel) was the birthplace of the Jewish people. Here their spiritual, religious, and political identity was shaped. Here they first attained statehood, created cultural values of national and universal significance, and gave the world the eternal Book of Books (the Bible).

Jews strove in every successive generation to reestablish themselves in their ancient homeland. They made deserts bloom, revived the Hebrew language, built villages and towns, and created a thriving community, controlling its own economy and culture, loving peace but knowing how to defend itself.

Politics in Israel

The Prime Minister is the head of the Israeli government. He or she is elected by the members of the Knesset, Israel's national legislature. The Knesset has 120 haverim (members). Since the voting in the Knesset is along party lines, the Prime Minister is always a member of the Knesset's majority party.

The 120 haverim of the Knesset are elected by the Israeli people. All citizens of Israel have the right to vote, including the country's Arabs, who make up 15 percent of the population.

The two largest political parties in Israel are the Likud and the Labor Party. There are also many smaller parties. Each of them reflects the interests of a different segment of the population. The dizzying variety of voices and choices often makes Israeli elections confusing. Very often no party wins a majority in the Knesset. In such cases the party with the most votes forms an alliance, or coalition, with several other parties.

Israelis do not vote directly for the candidate of their choice. Instead they vote for the candidate's political party. Each party has a list of candidates. The more votes a party gets, the more haverim it has in the Knesset.

The members of the cabinet are chosen by the Prime Minister. Just as in America, the members of the cabinet head the different government departments, such as defense, health, education, and religious affairs.

The President (Nasi) of Israel is elected by the Knesset. This position is mostly a ceremonial office. The President appoints judges, signs the new laws that the Knesset enacts, and greets foreign dignitaries.

David Ben-Gurion (1948–1953) was the first Prime Minister of Israel. Golda Meir was the sixth Prime Minister (1969–1974), and the first woman to hold this office. In 1992 Yitzchak Rabin was elected the ninth Prime Minister of Israel.

The Knesset building in Jerusalem. The Knesset is the legislative body of the State of Israel. Its 120 members are elected by a secret ballot.

Seventh Prime Minister of Israel
Menachem Begin (1913–1992)

Begin headed the Betar movement in Russia before he was 20 years old. Because of his Zionist activities, the Russians sentenced him to a Siberian labor camp. In 1942 he immigrated to Palestine, where he organized the armed Jewish underground struggle against the British. He evaded the police by disguising himself as a bearded rabbi. Begin founded the Herut (Freedom) Party and in 1977 became Prime Minister.

YITZCHAK RABIN (1922–)
Soldier and political leader
Rabin, a soldier turned politician, stunned the world when he signed a peace treaty with the PLO, Israel's enemy. Born in Jerusalem Rabin graduated agricultural school and was ready to join a kibbutz when World War II erupted. He fought in the Haganah and eventually became chief of staff of the Israel Defense Forces.

Elections in Israel are a time for television commercials, newspaper ads. personal appearances, and lots of election posters. This wall of 1977 election posters features Shimon Peres, of the Labor Party, running against Menachem Begin of the Likud. Menachem Begin won the election and became the seventh Prime Minister of Israel.

Rabin was the chief planner and directed Israel's stunning victory in the Six-Day War. Golda Meir, recognizing his leadership qualities, appointed him ambassador to the United States.

In 1974 he was elected Prime Minister but was forced to resign after three years. His second premiership began in 1992, and in September 1993 he signed the peace treaty with the PLO. Yitzchak Rabin wants history to record him as the architect of peace in the Middle East.

ISRAEL'S PRESIDENTS

Chaim Weizmann (1949–52) Zionist leader, prominent scientist.
Yitzhak Ben-Zvi (1952–63) head of the Jewish Angecy, historian.
Zalman Shazar (1963–73) politician, scholar, historian, author, poet.
Ephraim Katzir (1973–78) renowned biochemist.
Yitzhak Navon (1978–83) politician, educator, author.
Chaim Herzog (1983–1992) attorney, general, diplomat, author.
Ezer Weizmann (1993–)

ISRAEL'S PRIME MINISTERS

David Ben-Gurion (1948–53)
Moshe Sharett (1954–55)
David Ben-Gurion (1955–63)
Levi Eshkol (1963–69)
Golda Meir (1969–74)
Yitzchak Rabin (1974–77)
Menachem Begin (1977–83)
Yitzchak Shamir (1983–84)
Shimon Peres (1984–86)
Yitzchak Shamir (1986–1992)
Yitzchak Rabin (1992–)

The Knesset in session.

The Histadrut

Israel's most powerful force next to the government is the Histadrut (General Federation of Labor). It was founded in 1920 by David Ben-Gurion and has grown into a huge multifaceted enterprise. The Histadrut is active in four fields—as a labor organization, and conducting commercial, social, and educational activities.

First and foremost, it is an umbrella organization that covers more than 40 different unions, ranging from government employees to teachers. It is also active in international labor conferences and offers specialized training to union members in different countries.

Commercially, the Histadrut manages kibbutzim, the Hamashbir chain of department stores, and the Tnuva food company, which markets the food products of the kibbutzim. It also owns Bank Hapo'alim, the workers' bank. Solel Boneh, a construction company that is active in Israel and internationally, is another Histadrut enterprise. Israel's largest bus line, Egged, is an important and profitable Histadrut activity.

Socially, the Kupat Cholim (Sick Fund) is the Histadrut's most important service. It provides quality medical care for its members through a network of regional hospitals and about 1,000 local clinics. As of 1992 the Kupat Cholim had about 2.5 million members.

Educationally, the Histadrut owns its own newspaper, *Davar*, and a publishing company, Devir. It also offers a great variety of courses for its members to upgrade their skills and educational levels.

Every Israeli, whether Jew, Muslim, or Christian, is eligible for membership in Histadrut.

Histadrut, which began in 1920 with around 4,000 members, is a perfect example of how government and unions, working together, can create a more caring society and a stronger, more vibrant country.

Mashbir Lazarchan in Tel Aviv. This department store chain is one of Histadrut's most successful enterprises.

A 1948 Histadrut poster issued after the War of Independence features the theme of physical labor and vigilance.

BERL KATZNELSON
(1887–1944)

Farmer and labor leader.
Berl grew up with dreams of aliyah and became a devoted Zionist.
When he was 22, Berl Katznelson moved to Israel. There he became a farmer and labor leader. Katznelson helped start the Israeli health-insurance fund, Kupat Cholim, so that everyone could afford decent medical care.

He became editor of the Labor party's newspaper, *Davar*, and was a founder of the Histadrut.

During the Nazi Holocaust, Katznelson worked to save Jewish victims. Under his guidance Jewish soldiers parachuted into Nazi-held territory to save survivors.

Beilinson Kupat Cholim hospital in Tel Aviv. This hospital provides a full range of medical services for Arabs and Jews alike.

The Solel Boneh cooperative is an arm of the Histadrut. It started in 1923 and is today Israel's largest construction company. One of Solel Boneh's first projects was the building of a road from Rishon Le-Zion to Rehovot. The back-breaking work was performed by men and women.

Egged bus station in Tel Aviv. The Egged cooperative is a member of Histadrut. Its name comes from the Hebrew word *egged*, which means "linked together." The name was chosen because it expresses the close bond between members of the cooperative. Egged has about 6,000 members and operates 4,000 buses over 3,000 scheduled routes. It is the world's second-largest bus company. In wartime Egged assists the Israel Defense Forces by transporting personnel and equipment.

Israel Defense Forces

Every country needs an army to protect itself against its enemies. Countries which are located in peaceful areas need only small armies. Those with enemies on their borders need large armies. Countries such as Israel that are surrounded by enemies are forced to organize large armies.

In Hebrew the Israeli armed forces are usually referred to as Tzahal, an acronym derived from the initial letters of the words Tzvah Haganah Le-Yisrael, which mean "Israel Defense Forces," abbreviated in English as IDF. Tzahal includes all three armed services: army, navy and air force.

At the age of 18 young men and women are drafted into Tzahal for three years. After this they serve about one month a year in the reserve forces. If an emergency breaks out, the reserves are then mobilized into army.

Israelis begin their military training while teenagers. At the age of 14 Israeli boys join the Gadna youth corps. In special camps the teenagers learn hand-to-hand combat and weapons handling. Girls receive military training in Chen, the women's corps. In wartime Chen members work behind the lines, freeing the men for fighting units.

Many Israeli farm settlements are located on the country's borders. After several months of training some soldiers choose to serve in the branch of Tzahal known as Nachal ("heritage, inheritance"). Nachal is assigned to the border settlements, where its members double as soldiers and farmers.

Jews from all backgrounds come to Israel as immigrants. Many of the new immigrants cannot speak, read, or write Hebrew. The army educates and unites the soldiers into one Jewish community. In addition, Tzahal trains the recruits in skills which can be useful in civilian life.

After the Six-Day War in 1967, France embargoed all arms shipments, including Mirage fighter planes, to Israel. At that point the leaders of Israel decided that they could not depend on foreign sources for armaments and would build their own weapons.

One of the most important projects was the development of a made-in-Israel fighter plane. This supersonic air-to-air fighter is called Kfir. The Hebrew word *kfir* means "young lion."

TERMS OF MILITARY SERVICE

COMPULSORY SERVICE

All eligible men and women are drafted at age 18. Men serve for three years, women for two.

RESERVE DUTY

Upon completion of compulsory service, each soldier is assigned to a reserve unit. Men up to age 51 serve about 30 days a year, which in times of emergency can be increased to 60 days or more. Single women are also liable for reserve duty.

CAREER MILITARY SERVICE

Any man or woman having completed compulsory service and meeting IDF needs may sign up for the standing army. Career soldiers are eligible for retirement after 20 years of service.

A unit of the Israel Defense Forces (IDF) on parade.

EMBLEMS OF THE ISRAEL DEFENSE FORCES

Emblem of the Army

Emblem of the Navy

Emblem of the Air Force

Emblem of the Paratroopers

Ranks in Israel Defense Forces
סימני הדרגית בצבא ההגנה לישראל

רב אלוף	אלוף	סגן אלוף
Rav-Aluf	Aluf	Segan-Aluf
Lieut-General	Major-General	Lieut.-Colonel

רב סרן	סרן	סגן ראשון	סגן
Rav-Seren	Seren	Segen Rishon	Segen
Major	Captain	First Lieut.	Lieut.

סימני הסמלים על השרוולים

רב סמל גדודי	רב סמל פלוגתי	סמל אפסנאי
Rav-Samal	Rav-Samal	Samal Afsanai
Reg. Sgt.-Major	Pelugati Company Sgt. Major	Quartermaster Corp. Sgt.

סמל	רב טוראי	טוראי ראשון
Samal	Rav Too-Ray	Too-Ray
Sergeant	Corporal	Private

An Israeli military factory which manufactures the Gabriel ship-to-ship missile. The Gabriel is extremely accurate. Several foreign countries have purchased the missile system for their navies.

The Jewish Religion in Israel

Israel is the land of the Bible, with numerous holy places and religious shrines. Israel is also the homeland of the Jewish people, with numerous religious divisions. Though the majority of Israelis are not strictly observant, they celebrate the Jewish holidays and follow the ceremonies of the Jewish lifecycle.

The American Reform, Reconstructionist, and Conservative religious movements have established educational institutions, research institutes, camps, kibbutzim, and synagogues. The Jewish Theological Seminary and the Hebrew Union College have established branches in Israel which train rabbis and Hebrew educators.

However, religious power is centered in the politically organized Orthodox community, as represented by several religious parties, such as the National Religious Party, which controls the chief rabbinates and associated agencies, Shas, Agudat Yisrael, and Degel Hatorah.

At the founding of the State of Israel in 1948, Israel's first Prime Minister, David Ben-Gurion, made an agreement with the National Religious Party to maintain the Turkish system whereby each religious community—Muslim, Christian and Jewish—would retain control of matters of personal identity, marriage and divorce and related matters in their respective communities, with government support.

But the Orthodox communities are hardly united either politically or religiously. They are divided geographically, primarily into Ashkenazim and Sephardim, each with its own chief rabbi.

But each of these is further subdivided into the various Hasidic sects, such as the Gerrer, the Vizhnitzer, the Belzer, and the Lubavitcher; into non-Hasidic groups such as the "Litvishe" associated with the Agudah and Degel Hatorah; the centrist Orthodox, who are often fervent Zionists; and the Oriental communities such as the Moroccans, Iraqis, Egyptians, and Yemenites.

The more conservative members of these groups—the haredim—are perhaps more familiar to most American Jews, with their distinctive black garb, white shirts, beards and side-curls, or, for the women, their long skirts and long-sleeved blouses, wigged or covered heads. Despite this image, the Orthodox communities in Israel follow various lifestyles and occupations, from manual laborers and storekeepers to professionals and religious students and leaders.

The haredim refuse to speak Hebrew or to serve in the army. They believe that there should not be a Jewish state in Israel until the Messiah comes. To the Hasidim among them, Hebrew is the Holy Tongue and should only be used for prayer and Torah study. Instead they speak Yiddish.

There are Hasidic communities in many of Israel's cities, where their special religious and everyday needs are met. The largest Hasidic district, Meah Shearim, is in Jerusalem. The district was given the name Meah Shearim ("100 Gates") when it had its own defense system with 100 gates. Signs throughout the district alert visitors to the Hasidic dress code and style of behavior. Women are cautioned to wear modest clothes.

Hasidim in traditional garb. The fur hats are called streimels. The round hats were part of the Hasidic uniform in the ghettos of Europe.

A wall painting from the third-century C.E. synagogue at Dura-Europos, Mesopotamia. This painting illustrates a story from the Book of Samuel. The Philistines captured the Ark of the Covenant and brought it into the temple of the idol Dagon. In the morning, to their surprise, they found that Dagon had toppled to the ground before the Ark of the Covenant.

This wall painting represents the triumph of the God of Israel over the idol worshippers.

Street signs in the district of Meah Shearim in Jerusalem.

The two Hasidim wrapped in their tallits are hurrying to the early morning minyan in Meah Shearim in Jerusalem.

Israel Celebrates Holidays

In Israel the Jewish holidays and festivals are not just religious occasions but also national holidays. Schools, banks, and businesses close down on Rosh Hashanah, Yom Kippur, Sukkot, Passover, and Shavuot, as well as on all other Jewish holidays.

Besides the festivals celebrated by Jews all over the world, there are holidays which are special for the Jews of Israel. These festivals celebrate momentous historical milestones in the birth of the State of Israel.

Yom Yerushalayim, Jerusalem Day, is the newest holiday on the Jewish calendar. On this day, Wednesday, 7, 1967, after a bloody battle, Israeli commandos captured the Old City of Jerusalem. Battle-hardened soldiers wept as they prayed at the Western Wall.

On Yom Yerushalayim, 18 torches are lit on the Western Wall. These torches honor the memory of the heroes and heroines who made their final sacrifice in the fight for freedom.

Israelis celebrate this holiday with parades and parties. In the synagogues special prayers are recited.

Yom Hazikaron, the Day of Remembrance, is a sad day. Israelis remember their sons and daughters, fathers and mothers and relatives who died in battle or were murdered by Arab terrorists. The celebration starts on the evening of the 3rd of Iyar with the blast of sirens. A parent whose child died in the defense of Israel presents a torch to the President, who lights a flame in memory of the fallen Israelis.

At noon on the 4th of Iyar, sirens are blown and the whole country comes to a standstill in memory of its fallen heroes. A special ceremony in their honor is held on Mount Herzl.

Yom Ha'atzmaut, Independence Day, is celebrated on the 5th of Iyar. On May 14, 1948, after centuries of struggle, the State of Israel was officially established. This joyous holiday is celebrated with parades, singing, dancing, and prayer, and lots of fireworks.

Jews all over the world also celebrate Yom Ha'atzmaut with parades and special religious ceremonies.

An Israeli poster issued in 1990 to commemorate the 52nd birthday of the State of Israel. It announces that 1990 is the year of the Hebrew language.

The Yad Vashem Memorial: Ohel Yizkor—Hall of Remembrance. The walls are built of large, unhewn black lava rocks. On the mosaic floor are inscribed the names of the 21 largest concentration camps, and near the wall in the west burns a light.

Since 1948, the Israeli Post Office (Do'ar Ivri) has produced more than 600 postage stamps on various subjects.

The Jewish holiday stamps are especially colorful and extremely well designed. Pictured below are just a few of Israel's holiday stamps.

Israeli stamp issued to commemorate the liberation of the Nazi concentration camps by the Allies at the end of World War II.

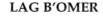

PURIM   PASSOVER   DAY OF REMEMBRANCE   YOM HA'ATZMAUT   LAG B'OMER   SHAVUOT

The Hebrew Language

Hebrew was spoken by our biblical fathers and mothers—Abraham and Sarah, Isaac and Rebecca, Jacob, Leah, and Rachel. The Torah is written in Hebrew; King Saul and King David, the great rulers of the Jewish people, spoke this tongue. The Hebrew language set the Jews apart as a proud, independent people who ruled themselves in their own land.

But in the year 586 B.C.E. the Babylonians conquered Israel. Some Jews always remained in the Holy Land throughout the generations. But many were exiled to Babylonia, where a rich and important Jewish community arose. Over the centuries, Aramaic, the language of Babylonia, became the spoken language of the Jewish exiles. When the rabbis of the Babylonian community recorded the Oral Law, they wrote in Aramaic and compiled the great work known as the Talmud.

In the year 70 C.E. the Romans conquered Israel and forced many of the Jews who remained there to leave. They sought refuge in the Jewish communities outside Israel, which were called the Diaspora, from the Greek word meaning "scattering" or "dispersion." To survive in their new homes in the Diaspora, the exiled Jews had to master the local language of the surrounding peoples—Italian, Polish, Russian, German, Spanish, Rumanian, Arabic to name a few.

Despite the exile, the Jews never forgot their homeland in Israel. They dreamed of the return to Zion (Shivat Zion) and the ingathering of the exiles (Kibbutz G'luyot). No matter what new languages they had to learn, one language forever remained at the heart of Jewish religious life—Hebrew.

Judaism kept Hebrew alive. Jewish prayer and Torah study kept the language vital. When the Jews finally returned to their beloved land in the late nineteenth century, the Hebrew language was restored as their daily language.

The process of updating Hebrew began with a man named Eliezer Ben-Yehuda, who is considered the "father" of modern Hebrew.

He refused to speak any language but Hebrew in his home and in the streets of Jerusalem. Arriving in Palestine in 1881, he established a school to teach Hebrew, compiled a Hebrew dictionary, and issued a weekly newspaper in Hebrew.

Ben-Yehuda invented new words for the many things Jews had to be able to talk about that were not around in the days of the Bible.

Some words were made from parts of the old Hebrew words. Others were taken from other languages and given a Hebrew sound.

Israel has established special language schools (ulpanim) which teach Hebrew to the thousands of new immigrants. The ulpan language program is a total-immersion experience. New Israelis live, work, and study together for at least four months, and only Hebrew is spoken, so the students are forced to learn their new language.

Today, Hebrew connects Jews throughout the world. The oldest and youngest of languages, the reborn Hebrew language is a treasure to be cherished by all Jews.

A class in Hebrew at the Bezalel School of Arts and Crafts in Jerusalem in 1906.

Israeli stamp commemorating the hundredth anniversary of the Hebrew Language Committee, Vaad Halashon Ha'ivrit.

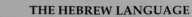

Table showing how the Hebrew and Phoenician letters passed through Greek and Latin forms to their present English form.

Special ulpan classes are available for new immigrants, where Hebrew is taught by methods designed for rapid acquisition of the language. These special classes are taught by the ulpan method.

Israel poster promoting the study of Hebrew.
The top two lines read: "One language—one people. For you and your children." The three bottom lines read: "Sign up today for evening lessons in Hebrew."

Israeli Schools

Israel is a country with a diverse population and needs a variety of educational tracks. The government has responded by establishing four different but equal types of schools: religious, nonreligious, yeshiva, and Arab. Israeli families can choose the schools that fit their needs.

All primary and high schools are free, and, like schools all over the world, teach the three R's—reading, 'riting, and 'rithmetic. However, since Israel is the Land of the Bible, Bible study is an extra basic subject. In addition, each school emphasizes the special aspects of its religious, social, and language programs.

Primary schools include grades 1–6, junior high schools are 7–8, and high school is a four-year curriculum. Arab children are taught in Arabic, and in the fourth grade also begin to study Hebrew.

The Israeli high school program is tough and competitive. Just as in most highly developed school systems, these schools have required courses and offer elective specialized courses of study. To graduate and become eligible for entry to college, students must pass a special exam called the bagrut.

The Hebrew word *bagrut* means "maturity." Students who pass the bagrut are considered mature enough to compete on the university level.

At the high school level, there are alternative trade and technical schools for those who do not wish to continue their academic studies. These schools teach a variety of skills, such as electronics, auto repair, nursing, and agriculture. These skills are vital for Israel's continued growth and future in a technical and competitive world economy.

Immediately after graduation from high school, the Israeli teenager enters the military service. Boys must serve three years, and girls two. By the time the Israeli reaches college, he or she is a 20-year-old military veteran. The older and more mature Israeli now has the choice of several excellent universities or yeshivot.

Some religious Israelis think of service in terms of Torah study. These Orthodox students attend a yeshiva, live in dormitories, and study together as one large family.

Israel is a small country with several high-quality universities that specialize in a variety of disciplines.

Ben-Gurion University is in Beersheba. It specializes in nature conservation courses and also has a medical school.

The Hebrew University of Jerusalem is Israel's oldest institution of higher learning. It boasts the finest medical school in the Middle East and has the best reputation of all universities in Israel.

Haifa is home to the Technion. It is a scientific powerhouse and specializes in high-tech and engineering studies. Postgraduate study also takes place at the Weizmann Institute in Rehovot.

Tel Aviv University and Bar-Ilan University are both in Tel Aviv. Bar-Ilan specializes in both academic and religious studies.

Overall, the Israeli school system is staffed by professional and innovative educators. New methodologies and teaching strategies are constantly being implemented .

Vocational training at a trade school in Israel.

Hebrew stamp featuring the Hebrew University in Jerusalem.

Israel is in the forefront of the educational revolution. A class in advanced computer technology at the Technion in Haifa.

Yeshiva students studying the Talmud.

UNIVERSITY ATTENDANCE IN ISRAEL AS OF 1993.

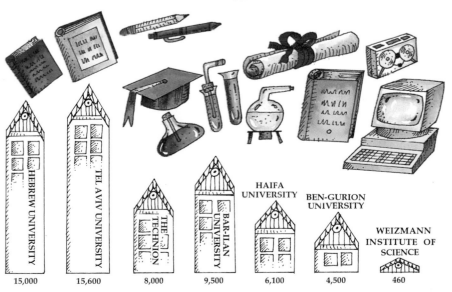

HEBREW UNIVERSITY	TEL AVIV UNIVERSITY	THE TECHNION	BAR-ILAN UNIVERSITY	HAIFA UNIVERSITY	BEN-GURION UNIVERSITY	WEIZMANN INSTITUTE OF SCIENCE
15,000	15,600	8,000	9,500	6,100	4,500	460

Books and Newspapers

It all started with that stubborn, single-minded Eliezer. Eliezer Ben-Yehuda rejuvenated the 4,000-year-old Hebrew tongue and created a modern language. He single-handedly laid the foundation for today's Hebrew culture. Today, Ben-Yehuda's spirit echoes through Israel's schools, theaters, TV studios, jazz concerts, computer programs, Hebrew newspapers and magazines.

As you would expect from the *am hasefer* ("people of the book"), the percentage of Israelis who buy books is one of the highest in the world.

Israel is an immigrant society, and its bookstores and newspaper kiosks reflect its diversity. Nearly every street in Israel has a newspaper stand or a bookstore overflowing with adult and children's books in a dizzying variety of subjects and in an amazing number of languages. Most Israeli homes have bookcases filled with books on art, religion, music, spy and historical stories. Books are the gift of choice for most occasions.

More than 2,000 titles are published each year. Every two years foreign publishers flock to Israel to participate in the Jerusalem International Book Fair, exhibiting their books and buying and selling publication rights. They buy permission to translate Israeli books for their own markets. Foreign publishers are eager to sell rights to translate their books into Hebrew. Publishers come in droves, since Israeli authors are well-known and their books are very popular. In 1966, the Israeli S. Y. Agnon won the Nobel Prize for literature.

Israel has more newspapers per capita than any other country. There are a total of 30 different daily newspapers. Twenty of them are published in foreign languages. Many of Israel's newspapers are published by political parties and follow the official political line.

The four most popular Hebrew papers are *Davar*, *Haaretz*, *Yediot Aharonot*, and *Maariv*. The *Jerusalem Post* is Israel's leading English-language newspaper. The immigration of Russian Jews to Israel has given birth to nine Russian newspapers. There are also papers in Ladino, Polish, Arabic, and other languages.

Every spring Hebrew Book Month is celebrated throughout the country with open-air markets. These markets are very well attended and customers fill the stalls looking for bargains.

Thanks to Eliezer Ben-Yehuda, the *am hasefer* is very much alive.

Every year during Hebrew Book Week, every large Israeli city turns its empty spaces into book markets. All publishers cooperate and sell their books at bargain prices.

HAYIM NACHMAN BIALIK
(1873–1934)
Greatest Hebrew poet of modern times Bialik's first poem was about his longing for Shivat Zion, the Return to Israel. Bialik supported himself as a businessman, teacher, and publisher.
In Israel today, Bialik is considered the national poet, just as Shakespeare is in English-speaking countries.

A montage of Israeli newspapers. A sampling of the names are: *Hadashot, Haaretz, Haboker, Maariv* and the English *Jerusalem Post*.

A sampling of Hebrew juvenile books. Some of these books were translated from other languages into Hebrew.

SHMUEL YOSEF AGNON
(1888–1978)
Nobel Prize winner
Agnon was an ardent Zionist. In 1907, at the age of 19, he moved to Israel (then called Palestine). He wrote stories about Jewish life, describing the people and places of his new home, modern Jerusalem.
Agnon received many awards, including the Israel Prize in 1954 and 1958. The crowning honor was the Nobel Prize for literature in 1966, the first granted to a Hebrew writer.

A 1965 Israeli stamp featuring the Jerusalem Book Fair.

Theater, Music, Art, Television

Despite its political and military problems, Israel has managed to produce an exciting and energetic home-grown culture. Israeli culture is a mixture of its 4,000-year history and the European and Middle Eastern world. Starting with the First Aliyah in the 1890s, the Jews of Israel have created a unique Hebrew world of literature, music, theater, art, radio, and television. Artists, musicians, dancers, sculptors, directors, and actors have combined their talents to entertain and educate the Israeli public.

The recent wave of Russian entertainers, artists, and writers has injected new energy and talent into the Israeli culture. There is something cultural for everyone and every occasion.

All of Israel's major cities have theaters which stage a variety of plays, ranging from original works to translations of foreign classics. Russian-language productions are very popular and play to sold-out audiences.

Israel's National Theater, Habimah, began in 1922. Today it presents three plays a day, six days a week. Needless to say, most of Israel's stage productions are extremely well attended.

Ever since the Levite bands performed in the Temple, the Holy Land has echoed with the sounds of music and song. For a tiny country, Israel has an amazing number of orchestras, ensembles, vocal groups, and dance bands.

Israel's major orchestra is the Israel Philharmonic Orchestra. It performs at its home base in the Mann Auditorium in Tel Aviv. This full-size world-renowned concert orchestra also travels around the country performing in army camps, development towns, and kibbutzim.

Pop concerts with visiting foreign and local artists are very popular. Tens of thousands of people turn out to listen to the visiting performers.

Throughout the country there are a large number of museums of every type and description. There are museums of art, science, and naval history, and of course museums featuring Bible artifacts.

The Rockefeller Museum in Jerusalem is the leading archeological museum in Israel. Some of the Dead Sea Scrolls are displayed in the Shrine of the Book in the Israel Museum in Jerusalem.

Tel Aviv has a Diamond Museum and a Diaspora Museum. The Eretz Yisrael Museum in Tel Aviv consists of eleven mini-museums constructed around the archeological site of Tel Qisale.

Israel is a news-hungry country, and many people carry transistor radios to keep on top of local and international happenings. Every hour is news time on Kol Yisrael ("Voice of Israel"). Taxi drivers, bus drivers, people in private cars, and even bicyclists turn up the volume so that passengers as well as pedestrians can hear the news. Israel's Kol Yisrael has three channels, each of which specializes in different programs: classical music, talk shows, and popular music. A special network broadcasts news in Arabic to Arab listeners in Israel and in Middle Eastern countries.

Almost every home has a TV set. Even Bedouin tents in the desert have tall antennas which catch Israeli, Jordanian, and

Syrian programs.

Daytime shows feature American soap operas with Hebrew titles and many foreign films. There are lots of variety shows, game shows, news and discussion panels.

All Israeli radio and television stations close for Shabbat and for the Jewish holidays.

Israel has a very exciting and varied art scene. Yaffo, Jerusalem, and Safed have large areas dedicated to artists, sculptors, and handicrafts.

There were many talented artists among Israel's earliest settlers. In 1906, Boris Schatz established the world-famous Bezalel School of Art in Jerusalem.

Israel's artists reflect diversity of background and training. Some are modern, some are abstract, and some are traditional. Israel's artists participate in international exhibitions, and some have had special shows in Paris, London, New York, and Rome.

Israeli stamp commemorating the 50th anniversary of Israel's radio network, Kol Yisrael.

BORIS SCHATZ (1867–1932)
Artist and founder of the Bezalel School.

In 1903, Schatz met Theodor Herzl. This meeting changed the course of his life and career, for Herzl inspired him to become an ardent Zionist and join his destiny with that of Israel. In 1906, Schatz went to Jerusalem to found the Bezalel School, now a world-famous art school where students learn painting, sculpture, calligraphy, and many forms of handicrafts. Schatz himself was a prolific artist who worked mostly in sculpture.

Israel Philharmonic concert in the Mann Auditorium, Tel Aviv.

Sports in Israel

Israel is a country in love with all kinds of sports. Israelis are especially enthusiastic about soccer and basketball. Israeli athletes are organized into several amateur basketball and soccer leagues which field more than 1,000 teams.

The oldest sports league is Maccabi. Another league, Hapoel ("The Worker"), is supported by Histadrut, Israel's labor union. Elitzur is the league for religious youth, and Betar is sponsored by the Herut political party.

All over Israel, fans keep their ears glued to the radio for the news of their favorite sports team. Games are very well attended, and championship events are always sold out.

Tennis, swimming, volleyball, and track are also gaining in popularity. Every city, town, and kibbutz has very well equipped sports centers where athletes can practice and play their favorite sports.

Every four years since 1932, Israel has staged the Maccabiah Games, in which Jewish sports champions from all over the world compete against each other.

Israel participated in the Olympic Games for the first time in 1952 in Helsinki. Since then it has taken part in all the Olympics. Israeli athletes participate in many events and have won a few medals.

In 1972, eleven Israeli athletes were murdered by PLO terrorists at the Olympic Games in Munich, Germany.

Specialized sports training for Olympic athletes, coaches, and athletes who represent Israel at international sports events is provided by the Wingate Institute of Physical Education. Its advanced training techniques have been copied by numerous international institutions.

Israel's most popular noncompetitive sports event is the Three Day March to Jerusalem. Thousands of people, of all ages, from all over the world, come to participate in this event. Schools, businesses, factories, families, and hiking clubs in other countries send teams to tramp through the Judean hills. The IDF sets up camps for the hikers where they can rest and repair their aching and blistered feet. The march ends with an enthusiastic parade through the streets of Jerusalem.

At Hanukkah time, there is a relay torch race from the graves of the Maccabees in Modin to the President's Palace in Jerusalem. The lighted torch officially starts the Hanukkah celebrations throughout Israel.

Israel's most popular beach game is called *malkot*. On every popular beach this paddleball game is played with much enthusiasm and lots of agility. The speeding, hard rubber ball has been clocked at 100 miles an hour.

Sports programs help keep Israeli children healthy and strong.

Palestinians, Israeli Arabs and Arabs from abroad participated in the Second Annual Jerusalem Marathon held in 1993. The winner was Hassan Saftaoui, a Muslim from Morocco.

The relay race from Modin to Jerusalem. The runners are passing a torch which will be handed to the President of Israel in Jerusalem.

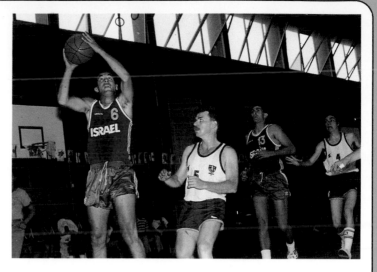

Israeli player scores against Greece in the 13th Maccabiah games.

Every year the Hapoel sports organization holds a country-wide competition. These Israeli stamps feature three sports in which the athletes compete.

Hanoch Bodian, a champship swimmer, who lost an arm in the Lebanese War, carries the torch to open the 13th Maccabiah games in Ramat-Gan Stadium.

Israeli stamp issued in honor of the 13th Maccabiah

The Kibbutz

In 1900 there were about 50,000 Jews living in what was then known as the Yishuv (Palestine). Half of them lived in the four holy cities: Jerusalem, Hebron, Tiberias, and Safed. The other 25,000 lived in several farming villages founded during the First Aliyah in the 1880s.

Zionists who dreamed of restoring the State of Israel were not happy with the slow pace of settlement. They searched for a way to increase the number of olim. After much debate they decided to found a new type of settlement called a kibbutz. The Hebrew word *kibbutz* means "to gather together," as in the term Kibbutz G'luyot, the Ingathering of the Exiles.

The kibbutz was a large farm community that operated as if all of its residents were one large family grouped together. All the members would work together, help each other, and share the benefits together. No one was to be richer or poorer than anyone else.

The kibbutz members (kibbutzniks) took turns raising and selling the crops, caring for the children, cooking and washing, and doing all the other necessary tasks, and all ate the same foods. The earnings of the kibbutz went into one bank account and were used for the benefit of all the members.

Kibbutz children were to be brought up by specially trained teachers. In some kibbutzim children slept in dormitories. All kibbutz members, in turn, worked in the fields, washed the dishes, drove the trucks and tractors, and stood guard at night against Arab attackers.

The first kibbutz, Degania, was established in 1909 in the Jordan Valley near the Sea of Galilee. The colony was founded by 20 young boys and girls on some swampy land bought from the Arabs by the Jewish National Fund. Today this tiny experiment has grown into a large farm and commercial enterprise.

By 1920, Degania had grown to the point where it was necessary to establish another kibbutz. Degania B was established near Degania A on land leased from the Jewish National Fund. Visitors to Degania A are now greeted by a Syrian tank—a souvenir of the War of Independence in 1948. It is a reminder of how the defenders of the kibbutz, a handful of men, women, and children, armed only with surplus rifles and homemade Molotov cocktails, defeated a Syrian tank column.

Degania is one of the most beautiful and successful kibbutzim. Together Degania A and B have a population of about 1,400 people. They raise a variety of agricultural crops and have four separate factories. In addition the kibbutz boasts an educational center, swimming pool, museum, guest house, and a small zoo.

Today there are about 300 large and small kibbutzim in Israel. They are no longer simply farming communities. Many of them have major food-processing plants and operate factories that manufacture a wide variety of industrial products.

Kibbutz Degania on the shore of Lake Kinneret.

Harvesting farm-raised fish at a kibbutz in Israel. Fish farming is an important and profitable industry in Israel.

In 1909 the Jewish National Fund bought a large tract of malaria-infested swampland in the Jezreel Valley. Kibbutzim Ein Harod and Tel Yosef were built in this valley. It is now one of the most fertile areas in Israel.

Taking care of the children in a kibbutz.

Fertilizing the kibbutz crops.

The Moshav

As of 1992, 90 percent of Israel's population live in the big cities and towns, and about 10 percent live on individual farms or in some form of farming community.

The kibbutz is a unique Israeli creation. But not everyone was eager to live in a community where there was no personal property, no money, and very little privacy.

On the other hand, the strength, money, and machinery needed to tame the wild, rocky, treeless, dry, diseased-ridden soil for farming made it impossible for the individual farmer to succeed on his own. The unstable security was another deterrent for the isolated farmer.

A solution to the problem was the moshav ovdim, or workers' settlement. The moshav combined the best of the kibbutz system—community ownership of farmland and equipment—with private land and house ownership.

A moshav consists of a large tract of community-owned land and individual plots for member families. The members own their own plots of farming or grazing land and their own houses.

The moshav operates on two separate levels; as individual enterprises owned by the members, and as a purchasing and selling agent for the group.

The moshavniks work their own land to raise fruit or vegetables or chickens or dairy cows. The farmer has access to the tractors, trucks, and farming machinery of the moshav. The profit or loss for their own enterprises belong to them.

The moshav acts as the farmer's agent. Because it buys for a group of farmers as well as for itself, the moshav gets cheaper prices. The moshav also markets the produce from the individual plots. Because of its greater productive capacity, it can better market its fruits, vegetables, or dairy products. Also, because of their size, some moshavim pack and process their own products and in that way increase their profitability. The profits and losses of the total moshav affect the individual moshavnik.

The first moshav, established in 1921, was Nahalal. Today, there are 300 moshavim in Israel.

The moshav shituffi is a variation of the moshav ovdim. The moshav shituffi, or collective settlement, allows no private farming at all. Members live as families in their own private homes. Everybody shares in the profits and losses. So far, there are only 20 of these moshavim in Israel.

The decline of agricultural profitability in Israel has caused serious financial problems for the moshavim and the kibbutzim. As a result, some have begun to diversify by establishing factories to increase their earning power.

Israel's kibbutzim and moshavim are models for developing countries wishing to solve their own growth problems. Observers and experts from all over the world stream to Israel to study its modern farming techniques. Israel's experts are welcomed by undeveloped countries who desperately need the agricultural knowhow to feed their undernourished and starving populations.

Harvesting dates on a moshav with a traveling electric picking machine.

A kibbutz house in Kfar Ha-Nasi in the Galilee.

Baling cotton at the kibbutz Kfar Ha-Nasi.

Aerial view of the moshav Nahalal. Private farms encircle the communally owned facilities.

A modern plywood factory on a moshav.

A Land of Milk and Honey

The Torah tells us that Israel was "a land of milk and honey." Ancient Israel consisted of a handful of urban centers and hundreds of widely scattered tiny towns and villages. The villagers earned their "milk and honey" working as farmers and shepherds.

In addition, the ancient Israelites were engaged in arts and crafts. The typical industries of the period were housed in small independent shops above or below the family quarters. Here skilled artisans crafted their products and sold them direct to the consumer.

The rebirth of modern Israel began about 100 years ago with a series of Zionist agricultural settlements funded by the Jewish National Fund and other charitable institutions. The first settlers knew nothing about farming but in a short time became agricultural experts.

Since gaining independence in 1948 Israel has become agriculturally self-sufficient. Its chief farm exports are fruits, flowers, and vegetables, especially for the off-season European and American markets. A large part of the agricultural produce comes from kibbutzim and moshavim affiliated with the four main labor organizations, the Histadrut (General Federation of Labor), Hapoel Hamizrachi (Religious Workers Co-op), Histadrut Haovdim (National Labor Federation), and Po'alei Agudat Yisrael (Orthodox Workers Co-op).

In addition to agriculture Israel's labor unions have also funded their own banks, insurance companies, newspapers, construction companies, sports organizations, health services and industrial enterprises. The kibbutzim and moshavim now earn about one half of their incomes from industrial output. Their products range from tools and plywood to pharmaceuticals and electronic appliances.

At one time, before 1960, Israel was classified as an underdeveloped country. Today, due to its exceptional advances, Israel is counted among the developed nations. Electronics, computers, lasers, armaments, pharmaceuticals and science-oriented industries are now supplying specialized equipment to the world market. In addition, Israel exports chemicals, textiles and polished industrial diamonds.

Despite all these economic advances Israel is forced to deal with two costly problems: defense and the massive influx of immigrants from Russia and Ethiopia. Large sums of money are needed to maintain an army and to purchase expensive military equipment.

In addition, the burden of the In-gathering of Exiles has added the cost of job training, housing, education and medical care to an already burdened economy. Grants by the United States and substantial support by Jewish sympathizers all over the world help ease the financial load.

On the horizon are two very significant events which are already making a dramatic change in Israel's economy. Thousands of highly educated Russian scientists and engineers have helped make Israel into a scientific paradise for research and development by multinational companies. Their knowhow has powered employment and Israeli industrial and scientific output. There are now numerous Israeli scientific oriented companies listed on American stock exchanges.

The peace treaty with the PLO also has the potential to trigger a rise in the Israeli economy. Israel hopes that the peace treaty will open the borders and promote free trade with its Arab neighbors. Unfortunately, the Arab boycott of Israel and against any company that does business with Israel is still in force. Despite the official boycott several Arab countries are quietly negotiating trade deals with their one-time enemy Israel.

Two Arab airlines are in the process of negotiations for passenger airline and landing rights. Israel's domestic airline, Arika, has signed an agreements for air service to Amman in Jordan and Damascus and Beirut. The moment peace is signed, these agreements will go into effect.

Of course the boycott harms the Israeli economy, but the Arab states also suffer. Israel has a sophisticated workforce of doctors, engineers, teachers and scientists which can help the Arabs. The Arab boycott denies jobs and trade and deepens the poverty and despair of their own people.

With peace Israel can once more fulfill the biblical dream of becoming a "land of milk and honey."

Emblem of the Israeli postal service.

Israel's money is divided into shekels and agorot. There are 100 agorot to a shekel. This is a 10-shekel bill.

Coins of 1, 5, 10, 25 agorot. There are
100 agorot to the shekel.

Ocean Transportation

The State of Israel is bounded by the Mediterranean Sea on the west and the Gulf of Eilat on the south. These bodies of water are highways for travel and commerce. They are also walls for Israel to protect itself from its enemies.

In biblical times King Solomon's ships regularly sailed from the port of Eilat to his trading partners in Africa and Asia. The Queen of Sheba landed in Eilat when she visited King Solomon in Jerusalem.

Israel's national shipping company is called Zim, a biblical word that means "ships." Zim was founded in 1945, three years before Israel's independence. It started operations with a small, dilapidated passenger ship called *Kedma*.

At first Zim's primary task was the transportation of hundreds of thousands of "illegal" immigrants from the refugee camps in Europe through the British blockade.

After independence the Arab boycott threatened to cut Israel's lifeline to the outside world. Once again, Zim's cargo ships were called upon to keep a steady flow of arms and military supplies for the Israeli armed forces.

From a fleet of old, rusty, leaky cargo ships, Zim has developed into a modern world-class shipping company. As Israel's industry has developed, Zim's modern cargo ships have reached out to new countries and ports. Ships proudly flying the flag of Israel sail from the cargo ports of Haifa, Ashdod, and Eilat. Israeli farm products and manufactured goods are carried to faraway ports in five continents.

Today Zim's modern ship-shape fleet consists of supertankers and modern container ships. These vessels regularly load and unload containers in most of the world's major ports.

The Bible tells us: "King Solomon built a fleet of ships at Etzion-Geber, which is near Elath, on the shore of the Red Sea, in the land of Edom. And Hiram [the king of Tyre] sent with the fleet sailors who were experienced with the sea, together with the servants of Solomon" (1 Kings 9:26–27).

King Solomon used Tyrian shipbuilders and seamen as well as his own sailors to trade with faraway countries. This stamp illustrates a re-creation of one of Solomon's merchant ships.

El-Al

Who would have believed that a plane decorated with a Magen David, flown by a Hebrew-speaking pilot, and serving kosher meals, would land in a Jewish country with its own airport while 400 Jewish passenger, tears in their eyes, sang the Hatikvah?

The country is Israel, the airport is Ben-Gurion, on the outskirts of Tel Aviv, and the airline is El-Al.

El-Al ("Skyward") is the State of Israel's national airline. It was founded in 1948 to transport Jewish DP's from the refugee camps in Europe to their new homes in Israel. This emergency fleet consisted of surplus planes flown by volunteers, Jewish and non-Jewish, from all over the world.

Since that first rescue, El-Al has been called upon to perform numerous similar missions. In 1949 its planes played a decisive role in rescuing Jews from Middle Eastern Arab countries. Thousands of Jews from Yemen, Aden, Morocco, Libya, and Algeria were flown to safety in Israel. Some of the planes were disguised with insignias from other countries.

In Africa during the 1980's, El-Al planes and pilots safely rescued more than 35,000 Beta Israel Jews from Ethiopia. Most of these airlifts were carried out in secret to foil the Arab terrorists who were ready to shoot down the planes with ground-to-air missiles.

Starting in 1986, Russian immigration has dramatically increased from a trickle to a flood of hundreds of thousands.

El-Al's high profile has made it a primary target for terrorists. Despite the constant threats, Israel's security precautions have managed to foil numerous attempts to plant bombs on El-Al planes.

Today, El-Al has a modern, well-maintained fleet of passenger and cargo planes with an excellent on-time record. El-Al's planes fly into most international airports, delivering passengers and cargo.

An El-Al airplane.

Water in Israel

The Torah describes Israel as the "land of milk and honey." In truth Israel is a poor country with limited natural resources. Rich countries, such as the United States, have many natural resources to meet the needs of their people.

The United States has fertile land for farming, minerals for mining, forests for lumber, oil for transportation, and water for drinking and farming.

Israel has few of these resources for its people. Almost no minerals, no oil fields, a few recently replanted forests, and a limited supply of fresh water.

Water is the key resource for farming and for industrial development. Neither plants nor animals nor people nor factories can exist without a good supply of fresh, clear water. Israel's water sources are limited.

The Middle East, with its long, dry summers, is a thirsty part of the world. The Jordan River and its tributary, the Yarkon, is Israel's only important river. The Jordan River is 186 miles long. It starts at the top of Mount Hermon. Melted snow from the mountain forms the Jordan River, which then flows into Lake Kinneret (the Sea of Galilee). From there the Jordan flows into the Dead Sea.

Lake Kinneret is also an important source of water. Look at the map on page 11 and you will see the that the lake gets its water from the Jordan River.

The Israelis have built a giant concrete pipeline called the National Water Carrier to distribute the scarce water supply. The National Water Carrier brings water from the Sea of Galilee into the dry Negev.

Where nature has failed to provide water sources, Israel even in biblical times found a way to provide water for drinking and farming.

The ancient Israelites dug deep holes plastered with clay, called cisterns. During the rainy season, in the winter, water was channeled into these cisterns. During the dry summers, this water was used for drinking and farming.

The Nabateans were an ancient non-Jewish people who were experts at water conservation. Some of their dams and cisterns have been found in the Negev and are even in use today.

Israeli scientists have also pioneered the use of desalinization plants. This expensive process uses salty Mediterranean water and turns it into sweet, drinkable water. Wells, pipelines, dams, cisterns, and desalinization plants have all helped Israel to found a prosperous modern economy.

The National Water Carrier also draws water from aquifers that run beneath the Gaza Strip and the West Bank. An aquifer is an underground layer of rocks that can store large quantities of water. Shallow aquifers can be replenished by winter rains. Deep aquifers cannot be replenished because of their depth. The water in deep aquifers was accumulated many years ago when weather conditions were much different.

The 1993 peace agreement with the PLO has brought the issue of water rights to the head of the peace table. No one, Israeli or Arab, is prepared to do with less water so that the other side can have more.

In 1953, the Eisenhower administration negotiated an agreement between Israel, Jordan, Lebanon, and Syria on sharing water from the Jordan and Yarmuk rivers. This agreement was never ratified by the Arabs, since doing so would have meant recognizing the right of Israel to exist. However, the peace agreement on Palestinian self-rule has now forced Jordan, Lebanon and Syria to seek such an accommodation.

As the Palestinians are given autonomy, Israel will have to negotiate its access to the Jordan River and the deep aquifers under the Gaza Strip and West Bank. Currently, Israel draws about one-third of its water from these aquifers.

Any peace treaty with Syria will have to consider the water supply which emanates from the Golan Heights. The water sources for the Jordan and Yarmuk rivers are in the Golan Heights.

The Romans were brilliant engineers and prolific builders. They left their imprint on the civilizations of the countries they conquered. Many Roman roads, monuments, aqueducts, and amphitheaters have survived the ravages of time and war.
This is one of the high-level aqueducts built by the Romans in Caesarea. It brought water from the local spring to the city.

Soldier opening the valve of an irrigation pipe at a new Nahal (army) settlement in the Aravah.

The National Water Carrier from Lake Kinneret to the south was completed in 1964.

Israel has developed a highly sophisticated irrigation system which can be assembled like a tinker toy. Here a farmer is bringing a long length of plastic irrigation pipe to a freshly plowed field for assembly.

Archaeology

The word "archaeology" is made up of two Greek words—*archaeo*, which means "old," and *logos*, which means "knowledge." Archaeologists dig the earth for knowledge of the old. They search for ancient pottery, scraps of letters, old coins, ancient weapons, perfume bottles and pots and pans, and human garbage. Like a detective the archaeologist examines the evidence and tries to hear the story that each object tells about the past. Archaeologists use many tools in their search for ancient knowledge.

A place may be inhabited for thousands of years. Old buildings are destroyed and new houses are built on top of them. In time a hill is formed. In Hebrew and Arabic a hill of this kind is called a *tel*. There are many tels in Israel. The ancient tools and other items found in them show us how our ancestors lived long ago.

When a tree dies, C-14 (radioactive carbon) slowly leaves the plant. By measuring the amount of C-14 scientists can figure out when the tree was born and when it died. In this way, they can work out the age of anything that was made of wood.

Ancient coins also help archaeologists find out about the past. The inscription on a coin may tell a story. For example, a Roman coin was found in one of the excavations. The writing read, *Judaea Capta*, which means, "Judea has been captured." The words were intended as a commemoration of the Roman capture of Jerusalem in 70 C.E.

Israel is an excavation-mad country. Archaeology is a national pastime for thousands of Israelis. Israel has a 4,000-year history. Cities and towns have been burned and destroyed. There are many hidden treasures which have been found and will be found in the future.

The famous Dead Sea Scrolls were accidentally found in the Qumran caves by two Arab shepherd boys. These scrolls were written thousands of years ago and have provided a look into the life of the ancient Israelites during Second Temple days.

The fortress of Masada is not just another archaeological site. It is an important chapter in the history of the Jewish people. Under the direction of the Israeli government, the ancient fort is being rebuilt. Archaeologists have uncovered the synagogue and discovered parts of hidden Torah scrolls.

In the caves of the Judean desert, archaeologists have discovered the letters of an ancient Israelite hero, Shimon Bar Kochba. The letters read "Shimon Bar Kochba, leader of Israel." The letters also tell about lulavim and etrogim for Sukkot. They were written during the second Jewish revolt against Rome in 132 C.E., when Judea briefly regained its independence under the leadership of Bar Kochba.

Every year exciting new discoveries about our ancient past are being discovered.

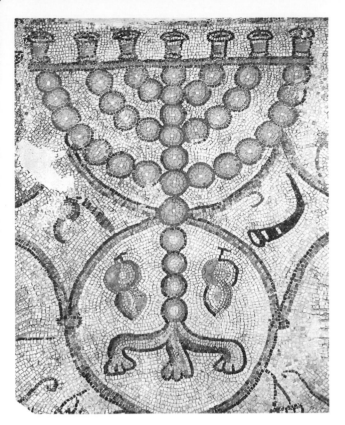

A relief is a deep carving on a flat surface. This stone relief of the Holy Ark was found in the ancient synagogue at Capernaum. The carving is about 2,500 years old.

A panel of the mosaic pavement from the fourth-century C.E. synagogue of Hammat Tiberias. The panel shows a menorah, a shofar, and other Jewish symbols.
At the time of the synagogue's existence, Tiberias was the seat of the Sanhedrin.

The mosaic floor of the synagogue at Bet Alpha. The round panel shows the symbols of the zodiac. The names are in Hebrew. This mosaic is about 1,500 years old. A mosaic is a picture made by placing small pieces of colored glass or stone in cement.

Every part of Israel is an archaeological treasure chest. Every hill and valley has a history dating back thousands of years. These young archaelogists are painstakingly excavating a historical site.

The Dead Sea Scrolls

Over the centuries, many of the books that our ancestors wrote and studied have been lost and forgotten. From time to time ancient books are found. They add to what we know about the beginning of the Jewish people.

In 1947 a great discovery was accidentally made by two Arab shepherd boys near the Dead Sea.

One day the two boys were watching their goats in the desert near the Dead sea. One of the goats wandered away. The two boys searched among the rocks and caves for the lost goat. Suddenly, one of the boys noticed a cave hidden by desert bushes. "Perhaps our missing goat is hiding in the cave," he shouted. "Let's search the cave."

They carefully approached the hidden cave. As they entered, thousands of bats drove them back into the sand. The frightened boys threw rocks at the bats. One of the stones hit something inside the cave that seemed to break.

The Arab boys ran away without finding the goat. The next morning, with new courage, the boys climbed back into the cave. On the dusty floor they found eight huge clay jars.

Inside the jars were many parchment scrolls. The scrolls were very old, but they had been preserved because of the dry climate in the Dead Sea area.

This accidental discovery is known as the Dead Sea Scrolls. The scrolls have told us many new things about the beginning of the Jewish people.

One of the scrolls is part of the Book of Isaiah.

The Dead Sea Scrolls are the oldest Hebrew manuscripts ever found. Some of the Scrolls are kept in the Shrine of the Book in the Israel Museum in Jerusalem.

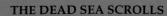

The Shrine of the Book is a part of the Israel Museum.

The Dead Sea Scrolls are the oldest Hebrew manuscripts in existence. They are housed in the Shrine of the Book, in the Israel Museum, Jerusalem. The scroll of Isaiah is displayed fully opened around a drum.

The fortress of Masada, high on a rock near the Dead Sea, was the last Jewish stronghold to fall to the Roman conquerors following the destruction of the Temple in 70 C.E.

Close-up of a Dead Sea Scroll.

Ancient jars found in caves at Qumran, containing some of the famous Dead Sea Scrolls.

The Synagogue in Israel

The synagogue is the most important institution in Jewish religious life. It originated during the Babylonian exile in 586 B.C.E. When the exiled Jews were permitted to return to Eretz Yisrael in 538 B.C.E., they brought back the practice of worshipping in synagogues.

During the time of the Second Temple, there were many synagogues in Israel, including one on the Temple Mount. When the Second Temple was destroyed in 70 C.E., the synagogue assumed a new role as a *mikdash me'at,* or small Temple. Many of the rituals of the Temple were transferred to the synagogue, and prayer became the substitute for sacrifices after the destruction of the Temple.

Archaeologists in Israel have unearthed many ancient synagogues. The synagogue at Capernaum (Kfar Nahum) in the Galilee is one of the largest. This fourth-century synagogue was built entirely of stone.

In 1928, the members of Kibbutz Bet Alpha uncovered an ancient synagogue from the sixth century C.E. Archaeologists discovered a beautifully inscribed mosaic floor with a zodiac circle. It contained colored panels of animals, flowers, and biblical scenes.

The city of Safed contains two interesting old synagogues. Throughout the Middle Ages Safed was a center for Torah study.

Rabbi Isaac Luria, called Ari ("lion") by his followers, came to Safed in 1568. After his death, during a plague in 1572, his followers built a synagogue where they would gather to welcome the Shabbat. This synagogue was destroyed in the earthquake of 1852.

The rebuilt synagogue has a shrapnel hole from an Arab attack during the 1948 War of Independence.

Rabbi Joseph Caro arrived in Safed in 1535. His most widely known work was the *Shulchan Aruch*, the Code of Jewish Law. His synagogue was destroyed in the earthquake of 1837, and was rebuilt in 1847. The ark contains three ancient Torah scrolls: a 200-year-old Persian Torah, a 300-year-old Iraqi Torah, and a 500-year-old Spanish Torah.

Jerusalem is a holy city and is home to many synagogues both ancient and modern. One of the major attractions of the Hebrew University in Jerusalem is the Hecht Synagogue. The synagogue has a very modern, outstanding architectural form.

Hechal Shlomo ("Palace of Solomon") in Jerusalem is the seat of the Orthodox rabbinate. The Great Synagogue is part of the Hechal Shlomo complex.

Israel is the land of the Jews. There are more than 1,000 synagogues in Israel. Every city, town, and village has at least one synagogue. As new immigrants arrive, more synagogues are being built.

Many Jews hope and pray that someday in the near future, the Holy Temple will once again be rebuilt on the Temple Mount.

Tiferet Israel synagogue in the Old City of Jerusalem. It was built in 1870 and destroyed during the War of Independence in 1948. Tiferet Israel means "The Glory of Israel."

The interior of the synagogue in Hechal Shlomo. The Hechal Shlomo complex houses the offices of the Chief Rabbis. The building is covered with white marble along the lines of Solomon's Temple. Hechal Shlomo means "Solomon's Mansion."

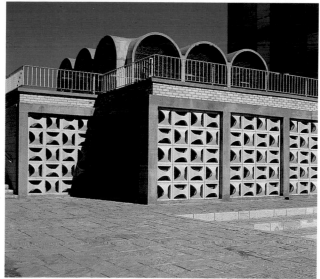

Exterior view of the synagogue in the Hadassah Medical Center. The synagogue features the famous Chagall Windows. Each of the 12 stained-glass designs pictures the symbol of one of the tribes of Israel.

The remains of the synagogue at Capernaum on the shores of the Sea of Galilee.

The Jewish Ancestors

The history of the Jewish people started with the founding fathers (patriarchs) and mothers (matriarchs) in the land of Canaan: Abraham, Sarah, Isaac, Rebecca, Jacob, Rachel, and Leah.

Abraham and Sarah came to Canaan, which today is called Israel, from Haran.

Jacob and his family, during a famine, traveled down to Egypt, where the Israelites were enslaved by Pharaoh. After much suffering they were freed by Moses.

Moses led the Israelites through the desert for forty years. He brought the Torah and the Ten Commandments down from Mount Sinai. The Torah guides the Jewish people in their daily lives.

Joshua inherited the leadership of the Israelite tribes. He led them across the Jordan River and began the conquest of Canaan. Each of the twelve tribes settled in a different part of Canaan and ruled itself.

When enemies attacked, leaders called *shoftim* (judges) united the tribes. One of the shoftim was Deborah. She was a prophetess and a great military leader. Deborah helped to defeat the Canaanites.

The prophet Samuel anointed Saul as the first king of Israel. Under his leadership the separate tribes united into one nation. He organized an army and led the war against the Philistines.

After Saul was killed by the Philistines, David became king. David made Jerusalem the capital of Israel. Under his strong rule the Israelite kingdom expanded and became very powerful.

When David died, his son Solomon became king. Solomon was a great builder. He built the magnificent Holy Temple in Jerusalem. Hiram, the king of Tyre, now called Lebanon, sent materials and craftsmen to help build the Temple.

The Cave of Machpelah, where the patriarchs are buried, is behind the ancient walls of Hebron.

Hebron was David's capital until his conquest of Jerusalem. There was a Jewish community in Hebron during most of the Middle Ages and through the Turkish period. The modern Jewish community of Hebron was destroyed by Arabs in 1929 and again in 1936. In 1929, 60 men, women and children were murdered by Arabs. Hebron was incorporated into Jordan from 1948 to 1967. It came under Israeli control during the Six-Day War, when the West Bank territories were conquered. In 1968 a new Jewish settlement was established just outside of Hebron. The settlement is called Kiryat Arba.

A wall painting from about 1900 B.C.E. in an Egyptian tomb. This beautiful painting shows a group of Semites bringing gifts to the Egyptians.

The Kingdom is Divided

Solomon died in 940 B.C.E. After his death the kingdom was divided. The southern kingdom, called Judea, was headed by Rehoboam, Solomon's son. The northern kingdom, called Israel, was headed by Jeroboam.

The northern kingdom consisted of ten tribes. Its capital was the city of Samaria. Jeroboam was chosen as its king.

In 722 B.C.E, when the Assyrians captured Samaria, the northern kingdom came to an end. King Shalmaneser V enslaved the Israelites and scattered them throughout the Assyrian kingdom. As a result, the ten tribes of the northern kingdom are known as the "lost tribes."

In the south, Judea consisted of only two tribes, Judah and Benjamin. Its capital was Jerusalem. Rehoboam succeeded his father Solomon as king.

In 701 B. C. E. Sennacherib, the king of Assyria, laid siege to Jerusalem. Guided by King Hezekiah and the prophet Isaiah, the people of the city withstood the enemy. However, as the siege wore on, food became so scarce in the city that surrender seemed inevitable.

Then an unexpected miracle came to the rescue of the besieged city. A terrible plague struck the Assyrian camp. Thousands of Assyrian soldiers died in the epidemic. His army greatly diminished, Sennacherib withdrew from Jerusalem.

The prophet Isaiah mourned for the ravaged land of Judah. Towns and cities were burned or lay in ruins. Yet, even in the midst of the ruins there were prayers of thanksgiving for the people who had survived the Assyrian onslaught. Before them now lay the great task of rebuilding the ravaged land. In haste they set to work, rebuilding their towns, replanting their fields, and tending their vineyards.

This stele (monument) was erected in honor of King Mesha of Moab. The language is Moabite. The inscription tells how Mesha won his freedom from the Israelites led by King Omri.

An obelisk is a four-sided stone monument which comes to a point. This obelisk was erected in honor of Shalmaneser III, king of Assyria. One of the panels shows King Jehu of Israel surrendering to the Assyrian king. Jehu is on his knees, bowing before the victorious Shalmaneser.

The First Return

In 586 B.C.E., the Babylonians under King Nebuchadnezzar invaded Judea. On the 9th day of Av, after much fighting the Babylonians captured Jerualem and destroyed the Holy Temple.

King Zedekiah was blinded and removed to Babylonia, where he died.

Thousands of Judeans were captured and marched in chains to Babylonia as prisoners.

As they were led in chains to a life of captivity in Babylon, the Jewish exiles sadly sang, "If I forget you, Jerusalem, may my right hand lose its cunning; may my tongue stick to its palate." They mourned for their lost freedom and their homeland in Israel. The idea of Zionism and the return to Israel started with the Babylonian exile.

More than fifty years later, in 539 B.C.E., the Persians defeated the Babylonians. Cyrus, the kind Persian king, allowed the Jews to return to Judea and rebuild the Temple.

The governor of this community was Zerubabbel. The Second Commonwealth, founded by the returning exiles, was called Judea. On the site of Solomon's Temple they began the work of rebuilding the Temple.

Unfortunately, the Edomites, Moabites, Ammonites and Samaritans attacked the poorly armed Jewish settlers. Despite the attacks the Jews continued to build the Temple. In comparison to Solomon's magnificent structure, the new Temple was very plain. However, the Levites and the priests still sang the same psalms and performed the same sacrifices and ceremonies.

Life in Judea was very difficult, and the Temple suffered from neglect. Among the Jews in Babylon who were distressed by Judea's troubled condition was the priestly scribe Ezra. King Artaxerxes of Persia gave Ezra permission to go to Jerusalem with his disciples. The king and the Jewish community in Babylon gave Ezra gifts for the Temple and supplies for the long journey. About 1,500 dedicated Jews accompanied Ezra to Judea. After a long trip they arrived in Jerusalem in 458 B.C.E. Without delay Ezra and his disciples began the task of teaching the people and bringing them back to the way of Torah.

The next major task was to protect Jerusalem against the enemy by rebuilding the wall around the city. Nehemiah, a Persian Jew, was appointed governor of Judea. He had been a trusted official in the palace of King Artaxerxes.

The armies of Babylon were defeated by the Persians. The Persians were good to the Jews of Babylon and Israel. They allowed Ezra and many Jews to return. Persian soldiers escorted the Jews. These are Persian soldiers. They are armed with spears and bows and arrows.

Nehemiah and Ezra combined their efforts to restore the commonwealth of Judea. Inspired by these two dynamic leaders, the people set about rebuilding the walls of Jerusalem. The Bible tells us that it took 52 days to rebuild the wall and fortifications of the city. Now hostile bands of raiders dared not attack the fortified city.

The revived Judea began to prosper. Farmers harvested in peace and shepherds were not afraid to tend their flocks. Once again traders came to buy and sell their products in Judea. Ezra and Nehemiah had reconstructed Jerusalem and revived the spirit of Torah in Judea.

During the exile, Aramaic replaced Hebrew as the everyday language of the Jews. There was a need for an Aramaic translation of the Torah when it was read in the synagogue. Congregations used interpreters to translate the Torah as it was being read. These Aramaic translations were called Targumim. Some of these texts are available today.

Inscribed cylinder recording the capture of Babylon by Cyrus. It tells how "without battle and without fighting Marduk [the god of Babylon] made him [Cyrus] enter into his city of Babylon; he spared Babylon tribulation, and Nabonidus the [Chaldean] king, who feared him not, he delivered into his hand." Nabonidus, the Chaldean king of Babylon, was not in favor with the priests, and they assisted in delivering the city to Cyrus.

Babylonia's most beautiful city was its capital Babylon. Babylon was graced with paved streets, gardens, temples and palaces. Even the city gates were adorned with multi-colored, glazed bricks.

This is a reconstruction of the Ishtar Gate in the city of Babylon. The designs of lions, bulls and dragons are made of baked bricks, covered with glazes of blue, gold and white.

Nebuchadnezzar invaded Judah and captured King Jehoiachin. King Zedekiah, who succeeded him, when Jerusalem was destroyed. This tablet, from the period of Nebuchadnezzar, tells about these events.

The Maccabees

In the fourth century B.C.E., Alexander the Great, king of the Greeks, defeated the Persians. Alexander's empire was like a difficult jigsaw puzzle which he had pieced together conquest by conquest. On his death, at the age of 33, his generals pulled it apart into separate little kingdoms.

In about 170 B. C. E., Antiochus IV, a descendant of one of the generals, became the ruler of Syria and Israel. He was very cruel and refused to allow the Jews to study Torah and to practice their religion.

The first stirrings of rebellion started one day in the small village of Modin, near Jerusalem. On that day Syrian officials and soldiers came to Modin to force the people to worship the Greek gods. There was an old priest in the village, a man called Mattathias, of the Hasmonean family. Mattathias, surrounded by his five sons, walked up to the heathen altar. A Jew who collaborated with the Syrians had just bowed to the idols. Mattathias raised his sword high. In a voice loud and clear he cried, "He who is with God, let him come to me!" then killed the idol worshipper.

The priest's bold act inspired his sons and followers. They attacked the Greek soldiers and officials and killed them. The revolt had begun!

Mattathias died soon after the beginning of the revolt, but his five sons vigorously took over his leadership. They gave the command to the third son, Judah, who was called Ha-Makkabi—the Hammerer.

Led by Judah Maccabee, a bold guerilla fighter, the Jews defeated the Syrians. The triumphant Maccabee warriors marched to the Temple in Jerusalem. A dismaying sight greeted them, for the Syrians had desecrated the Temple with idols. The victorious Jews set about clearing their house of worship.

On the 25th day of Kislev, 165 B.C.E., three years after its desecration, the Temple was rededicated. The Eternal Light and the golden menorah were lit once more.

Tradition tells us that the victors found only enough oil in the Temple to keep the Eternal Light burning for one day. Yet the Eternal Light and the golden menorah burned for eight full days.

The eight-branched hanukkiah of today and the annual eight-day celebration of Hanukkah, the Festival of Lights, commemorate the victory by Judah Maccabee and his courageous followers.

In Israel, Hanukkah starts with a torch relay race from Modin to Jerusalem. The lighted torch starts the holiday of Hanukkah.

An enameled picture of Judah Maccabee. It was painted in the 15th century by a French painter.

A Greek soldier under attack. He wears a metal helmet and breastplate. This painting was found on an ancient stone coffin.

A mosaic showing a likeness of Alexander the Great.

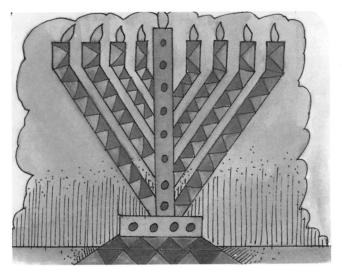

In memory of the miracle of Hanukkah, Jews light an eight-branched candelabra called a hanukkiah for eight days. The first night one candle is lit, and each following night one more candle is added until eight are burning brightly.

Jewish ritual objects, including two seven-branched candlesticks, are shown on the base of a gold goblet of the second century C.E. found in a Jewish catacomb in Rome, where it was hidden from the Romans. The objects shown on the goblet are believed to have been taken from the Temple in Jerusalem when it was desecrated by Antiochus IV of Syria in about 170 B.C.E..

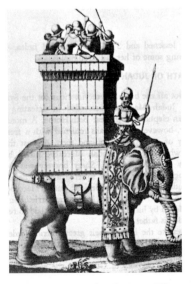

A Syrian war elephant. These huge beasts with sharpshooting bowmen were the armored tanks of the ancient world.

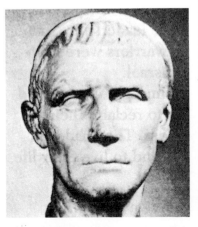

Marble bust of Antiochus IV.

The Second Temple

After Judah died, the Hasmonean family continued to rule Judea. For the first time in centuries, Judea was again a free and independent nation. There was a sense of freedom and prosperity in the land. Many of the citizens of Judea could read and write. Moreover, they were familiar with the Torah and its teachings.

After 100 years of peace, a religious split developed between two factions of the Hasmonean dynasty. At that point in history, Rome was the strongest power in the world. Foolishly, both parties appealed to Rome for help. Rome eagerly answered the summons and sent General Pompey to settle the argument. However, the Judeans paid the price of Roman intervention by losing their independence in 63 B.C.E.

The Romans appointed their own officials, called procurators, to rule the land. The procurators crucified thousands of Jews and stole all the gold and silver they could find. One procurator, Pontius Pilate, crucified the young Jewish preacher Jesus in about the year 30 C.E.

Because of these cruel policies, the land of Judea was in a state of unrest. A new Roman procurator called Florus was sent to bring peace to the country. Instead, he increased taxes and robbed the Temple treasury. Under the cruel Roman thumb the situation became intolerable for the Jews. The streets of Jerusalem were buzzing with talk of revolt.

In 66 C.E during the reign of the insane Emperor Nero, the Jews revolted. The Romans were forced to flee Jerusalem. Soon the Romans sent another army under the command of General Titus.

The Jews fought bravely, but were no match for well-equipped, powerful Roman legions. After much fighting they were pushed into their last stronghold, Jerusalem. There they made a last desperate stand for freedom. For weeks the outnumbered men, women, and children defended themselves against the Roman might. But in 70 C.E., on the 9th day of Av, the exact same day on which the First Temple was destroyed, the Romans set the city of Jerusalem and the Holy Temple on fire. Men, women, and children found inside the Temple walls were massacred.

Emperor Titus was so proud of his victory that he personally led a parade through the city of Rome. Chained Jewish prisoners were forced to carry the golden menorah and the Temple vessels through the streets of Rome. The Romans erected a huge monument to commemorate the victory. The infamous Arch of Titus still stands in the city of Rome.

In addition the Roman government struck commemorative coins with the words *Judaea capta*—"Judea is captured."

Jews mark the 9th day of Av (Tisha B'Av) as a day of fasting and mourning in memory of the martyrs who fought for Jerusalem in 70 C.E. Tisha B'Av also honors the memory of all Jewish heroes who struggled for freedom.

A small remnant of Jews escaped to Masada to continue the fight.

The carving on the Arch of Titus shows the menorah and other furniture of the Temple being carried in triumph through the streets of Rome.

To shame their unfortunate Jewish prisoners, Roman soldiers forced them to parade in chains through the streets of Rome carrying the captured Temple menorah.

The Romans felt so proud of this triumph over the Jews that they pictured the event on a monument called the Arch of Titus, named after the general who had captured Jerusalem. Today, the Arch of Titus still stands in Rome, and the carved picture of the Jews carrying the shamed menorah can still be seen. To the Romans, the story celebrated Roman might and triumph. To Jews, the story told of the loss of independence in their homeland.

This Roman coin, inscribed *Judaea Capta*, "Judea is captured," recalls the Roman victory in the first Jewish Revolt.

This fifteenth-century French painting shows Pompey and his soldiers desecrating and looting the Holy Temple.

Tisha B'Av is a day of fasting and mourning. The synagogue is lighted only by the glow of the Ner Tamid and memorial bulbs.

The service is sad and tearful. In some synagogues people sit on the floor and wear slippers or sneakers as a sign of mourning. At services a special book of the Bible is chanted. The Hebrew name of this book is Aycha. In English it is called Lamentations.

Masada

In the year 70 C.E., on the 9th day of Av, General Titus and his Roman soldiers set the Second Temple aflame. Those Jews who escaped the massacre were put in chains and taken to Rome to be paraded through the streets.

But the flame of freedom still burned brightly among the Jewish soldiers who had escaped the Roman legions. There was still one more stronghold, the fortress of Masada, where 960 Jewish men, women, and children had taken refuge.

Masada is a rocky plateau in the Judean desert overlooking the Dead Sea. The remarkable fortress on its flat top was built by King Herod around 37 B.C.E. Herod was hated by his subjects, so he designed Masada as a safe haven in case of revolt or invasion. He made Masada impregnable by digging cisterns for water storage and massive storerooms for food and arms. Around the perimeter of the fortress he built stone towers from which his soldiers could repel any attack.

For over two years the 960 heroic fighters in Masada refused to submit. In 73 C.E. the Romans decided to end the long siege. They built a wall around the fortress so that no one could escape. They brought up catapults which hurled stones and flaming oil-soaked missiles into the fortress. Roman engineers erected a long, sloping earthen ramp which led to the top of the mountain. All was in place for the final assault.

On the first day of Passover in 73 C.E., Elazar ben-Yair, the Jewish leader, called together all of the defenders. He said, "We know that tomorrow we shall fall into the hands of the enemy. But we still have the free choice of dying a noble death with our loved ones."

The next day, with a victorious shout, the Romans stormed the stronghold of Masada, but their victory was an empty one. There were no Jews left to massacre or to sell as slaves. All had died a heroic death.

The ancient site of Masada has been excavated by archaeologists, and a part of the fortress has been reconstructed exactly as it was during the siege. A treasure-trove of coins, weapons, cooking pots, and personal belongings of the defenders has been discovered. Among the artifacts were parchment fragments with the words "For the freedom of Zion."

This Hebrew sign atop Masada reads, "Masada will not fall again."
Graduation exercises for members of Tzahal who have completed paratroop school are conducted on Masada.

A silver shekel of the First Revolt dated Year Five (70 B.C.E.), found at Masada.

The fortress of Masada was built by King Herod. It has been excavated and a large part has been reconstructed.

Storage rooms at Masada.

The ruins of the synagogue on Masada. The round pillars in the center of the photograph supported the synagogue roof.

The battering ram was a very effective Roman offensive weapon. It smashed the defense walls and opened the way for the Roman infantry.

The Second Jewish Revolt

Years of peace followed the war against the Romans. Synagogues and schools were established in each community. Almost every Jew could read and write. But good things have a way of coming to an end.

Peace in Judea ended during the reign of the Roman emperor Trajan. Under Trajan's cruel rule revolts broke out in many parts of the Roman Empire.

His successor, Hadrian, continued the policies of Trajan. He built a temple with Roman gods in Jerusalem, a circus, and an arena where gladiators fought each other to death. Hadrian made it difficult to practice the Jewish religion. He decreed that any Jew studying the Torah would be killed. This the Jews refused to tolerate.

In 132 C.E. the Jews, led by Shimon Bar Kochba and Rabbi Akiva, once more revolted. At first Bar Kochba's army won many victories. His troops captured Jerusalem and built an altar on the Temple Mount.

Under Bar Kochba's leadership Judea had several years of freedom. Special coins were struck to commemorate Judea's independence.

However, Hadrian wanted to use Judea as a lesson for the other captive nations that made up the Roman Empire. He sent an army to Judea under the command of General Severus. One by one Severus destroyed the strongholds of the Jewish fighters. Bar Kochba and his warriors retreated to the mountain fortress of Betar, where they made their final stand. No water or food reached the Jewish soldiers, and many died of thirst and starvation. Bar Kochba and all of his soldiers died in the last battle defending Betar.

Hundreds and thousands of Jews were captured and sold into slavery throughout the Roman Empire. Jerusalem was renamed Aelia Capitolina and Judea was renamed Palestine, in order to blot out all memory of the connection between the Jewish people and the Holy Land.

On the holiday of Lag B'Omer we remember Bar Kochba and Rabbi Akiva, who sacrificed their lives for freedom.

RABBI AKIVA
(50 C.E.–135 C.E.)
Rabbi, Leader, Martyr
Rabbi Akiva, the great scholar, headed a yeshiva in B'nai B'rak. When the Romans outlawed Torah study and prayer services, Rabbi Akiva and his students continued to study and pray. Rabbi Akiva and Bar Kochba, together, organized the revolt against Rome. There were hundreds of thousands of Jewish casualties in the fight for freedom. Among the victims was Rabbi Akiva, whom the Romans tortured to death. Rabbi Akiva, 85 years strong, died a hero reciting the Shma prayer.

A silver coin issued by the revolutionary government of Bar Kochba. He and his followers set up a Jewish state (132–135 C.E.) which was soon crushed by the Romans.

In 1960, Yigal Yadin, professor of archeology at the Hebrew University in Jerusalem, launched an expedition to explore the caves in the mountains near the Dead Sea. A member of the expedition, exploring one of the narrow tunnels of a cave, discovered a basket filled with objects. Further inspection of the crevice revealed a treasure trove of artifacts which included sandals, knives, mirrors, jugs, bowls, and the greatest treasure of all—papyrus rolls containing about 40 letters from Bar Kochba.

In the letter shown here, Bar Kochba requests etrogim, lulavim, myrtles and willows—the "four kinds" needed for Sukkot.

The holiday of Lag B'Omer is celebrated on the 33rd day of the counting of the Omer. It is a time for singing, dancing, bonfires, picnics, hiking, and playing with bows and arrows.

On the holiday of Lag B'Omer Jews remember the heroes who fought the Romans. On Lag B'Omer Jews especially remember Rabbi Akiva's student Shimon Bar Yochai. Under Roman rule he and his students continued studying Torah in a cave high on Mount Meron. The students disguised themselves by carrying bows and arrows and pretending they were hunting so the Romans would not arrest them.

For 13 years Rabbi Shimon Bar Yochai kept the knowledge of Torah alive. This brave rabbi died on Lag B'Omer.

Today in Israel many Jews travel to Meron on foot and by car to visit the grave of Shimon Bar Yochai.

It is a tradition to sit around bonfires all night, telling stories and singing songs about Shimon Bar Yochai, Rabbi Akiva, and the hero Shimon Bar Kochba.

A Roman soldier with his combat equipment. The short sword was called a gladium and the shield was called a scutum.

The Romans developed a wooden catapult that could throw giant stones very far. Because of its kicking action it was called an onager. An onager is a wild donkey which defends itself by kicking wildly.

The Birth of Christianity

Christians view Israel as the Holy Land because Jesus was born there. They believe that Jesus was the Messiah. Jesus, whose Hebrew name was Jeshua, was born in the town of Nazareth during the period when Rome ruled Israel. He became a popular preacher and gathered a following among the villagers and fishermen who lived nearby.

The Roman authorities were suspicious of anyone who showed signs of leadership. They feared a revolt and worried that Jesus would incite his followers to rebel against Rome.

In the year 30 C.E., during the holiday of Passover, Jesus and his disciples went to Jerusalem. As far as the Romans were concerned, Passover was a very dangerous period. With so many Jews from all over Israel massed at the Temple for holiday services, they were concerned that a revolt might break out.

At the Passover Seder the disciples of Jesus officially proclaimed him as the Messiah. This increased the pressure and fear of the Roman governor, Pontius Pilate. He ordered that Jesus be captured and executed by crucifixion, the standard form of capital punishment used by the Romans. It is estimated that during this period thousands of Jews were crucified by the Roman authorities.

After the death of Jesus, some of his followers formed a small group to discuss and pass on the ideas he had taught them. They told stories about his life. The Christian religion developed out of this modest beginning.

Saul of Tarsus, a tentmaker who is more widely known by his Greek name, Paul, helped propel Christianity onto the world stage, where it spread like wildfire. Saul's far-ranging travels to Europe and Asia carried the message to the non-Jewish world and proved very successful.

Eventually the Christian religion became a world movement. The record of the life and teachings of Jesus, together with the letters of Paul and other early Christians, is known as the New Testament, in contrast to the traditional Hebrew Bible which in Christian eyes is the "Old Testament."

Today there are 120,000 Christians living in Israel, most of whom are Arabs. Armenian, Coptic, Anglican, Lutheran, Russian Orthodox, and Roman Catholic are just a few of the churches in Israel. These institutions enjoy complete religious freedom and have friendly relations with the government of Israel.

In 1994, the Vatican, representing Roman Catholics around the world, and the State of Israel established formal diplomatic ties and exchanged ambassadors.

רחוב הַנּוֹצְרִים

طريق حارة النصارى

CHRISTIAN QUARTER RD.

The old city of Jerusalem is divided into four sections or quarters: Jewish, Arab, Christian and Armenian. The Christian quarter contains many churches, schools and important historical and religious sites.

For five centuries, Rome dominated the ancient world. Among its conquests were Spain, France, England, Greece and the Balkans, Mesopotamia, Armenia, Egypt, Judea and North Africa. At its height, the Roman Empire controlled an expanse which included 100 million people.

The Roman armies were well-equipped and led by talented commanders. Success in battle came easily to this well-disciplined fighting machine.

These Roman soldiers belonged to the Praetorian Guard, the Emperor's personal bodyguards.

This limestone rock, excavated in Caesarea, is inscribed with a dedication to Pontius Pilate, the Roman governor who authorized the crucifixion of Jesus.

Street sign of Via Dolorosa. The inscription is in Hebrew, Arabic, and English.

Greek Orthodox chapel in the Church of the Holy Sepulchre in Jerusalem.

Beginning of the Via Dolorosa, a street in the Old City of Jerusalem. Church domes are in the background.

Mishnah and Talmud

When the Romans laid siege to Jerusalem, Rabbi Yohanan ben Zakkai thought of a plan to preserve the tradition of the Torah. He decided to start a school—an academy of Jewish learning—away from Jerusalem where the Torah could be studied and questions of Jewish law could be discussed.

Because of the Romans, it was impossible to leave Jerusalem. According to a tradition, Yohanan had his students spread the news that he had died. Yohanan had himself put into a coffin, and his disciples carried him out of the city.

Once he was out of the city, Yohanan ben Zakkai stepped out of the coffin, very much alive. When the scholars were stopped by a Roman patrol, Yohanan asked to be brought before their commander, Vespasian.

Yohanan predicted that Vespasian would soon be come emperor of Rome. Vespasian was very pleased by this prediction and promised to grant any favor that Yohanan might request.

After the destruction of Jerusalem, General Vespasian granted Rabbi Yohanan permission to set up a yeshiva in the coastal town of Yavneh. As soon as the academy opened, Rabbi Yohanan reestablished the Sanhedrin. This Jewish court consisted of 71 scholars who would decide questions of Jewish law and Torah scholarship. Rabbi Yohanan also instituted the practice of appointing rabbis to serve as the teachers who would continue to strengthen the long, unbroken chain of Jewish tradition.

After the second revolt against Rome, led by Bar Kochba, the academy was forced to move from Yavneh to Tiberias. Rabbi Yehudah Ha-Nasi, who now headed the academy, feared that the many oral teachings that elaborate and interpret the Torah would be lost and forgotten. The oral teaching had grown so large that no one could possibly remember all of it. With the assistance of his colleagues as students, Rabbi Yehudah Ha-Nasi arranged the entire Oral Tradition. This work was called the Mishnah. The Mishnah is divided into six main divisions, each one dealing with a different area of life.

In later generations the rabbis of Israel and Babylon compiled commentaries on the Mishnah. These commentaries are grouped together as the Gemara. The combination of Mishnah and Gemara is called the Talmud ("Learning").

The rabbis and scholars in the Land of Israel completed the Jerusalem Talmud in about 425 C.E.

The rabbis in Babylon completed the Babylonian Talmud in about 500 C.E. The Babylonian Talmud is recognized as more complete and authoritative than the Jerusalem Talmud.

DIVISIONS OF THE MISHNAH

Yehudah Ha-Nasi codified all the legal commentaries and decisions of the Oral Tradition according to subject matter, cataloguing them into the following six main divisions:

1. Zeraim (Seeds): laws concerning agriculture.
2. Mo'ed (Festivals): laws pertaining to the observance of the Sabbath, festivals and fast days.
3. Nashim (Women): laws concerning marriage and divorce.
4. Nezikin (Damages): civil and criminal laws.
5 . Kodashim (Holy Matters): laws concerning the Temple services, sacrifices, and Shehitah (Kosher slaughter).
6. Tohorot (Purities): laws of ritual purity and cleanliness.

The heading starts with the page number, the name of the chapter, the number of the chapter, and the name of the tractate.

Rashi, whose full name was Rabbi Solomon ben Isaac, was an eleventh-century French scholar. Rashi's commentary on the Talmud is one of the most influential contributions to rabbinic literature ever written.

The text of the Talmud consists of the Mishnah and the Gemara. The Mishnah is the six-part legal code which was developed in Israel during the first and second centuries C.E. It was written in Hebrew and was completed by Rabbi Yehudah Ha-Nasi.

The Gemara is written in Aramaic and is a summary of the legal debates on the meaning of the Mishnah. It was compiled in the Babylonian academies between the third and sixth centuries C.E.

המניח פרק שלישי בבא קמא   70

This commentary to the Talmud, called *Ayn Mishpat*, lists the sources of the laws and quotations cited in the Talmud. *Ner Mitzvah* lists the legal literature relevant to the talmudic passage.

The disciples of Rashi, called Tosafists, lived in the twelfth, thirteenth, and fourteenth centuries, and composed a talmudic commentary called Tosafot. The word "Tosafot" means commentary.

This is a commentary on the Talmud by Rabbenu (Hananel ben Hushi'el). Rabbenu lived in Kairouan, Morocco, in the tenth and eleventh centuries.

A page of the Talmud with some of the commentaries. The selection is from Baba Kamma, first tractate of the Order Nezikin.

There are numerous other commentaries in this edition of the Talmud, but they do not appear on this page.

The Crusades

Several times, during the Middle Ages, Christian Europe tried to take control of the Holy Land. The Muslim rulers had destroyed Christian shrines and killed the pilgrims who came to worship in the churches.

In 1095 a church council was held in France under the leadership of Pope Urban II. A Crusade, or "Holy War," was organized to free the Holy Land from the Muslim unbelievers.

The crusaders, wishing to spread Christianity, called themselves Bearers of the Cross, but in the name of religion they spilled much innocent blood. As they marched through Europe on the way to the Land of Israel, the crusaders attacked defenseless Jewish communities. High church and government officials tried to stop the slaughter, but the mobs could not be controlled. The memory of the Jewish martyrs who perished in these brutal attacks is immortalized in special prayers written during this period—the Av Harachamin service. These prayers ask God to avenge the death of the innocent Jews.

After a long march across Europe and Turkey the crusaders attacked the Land of Israel from the north. Other crusaders arrived by sea. The Bearers of the Cross, after bitter fighting, entered Jerusalem and slaughtered its inhabitants. The bloodthirsty crusaders murdered thousands of Jewish and Arab residents.

During the First Crusade, the Christians gained control of Jerusalem and ruled over most of the country. They built many fortresses. In 1138 the crusaders built the fortress of Belvoir in the Galilee. It was of great strategic importance since it commanded the crossing places over the river Jordan. But the Muslim foes did not remain quiet for long. Just 88 years after Jerusalem was taken by the crusaders, Saladin, the Muslim ruler, recaptured it. In 1291, the Muslims completed their victory by capturing Acco and putting an end to Christian rule in Israel.

There were a total of eight crusades, all of which, except the first in 1096, ended in defeat and death for the crusaders. The Fourth Crusade resulted in the capture of the Christian city of Constantinople. The Bearers of the Cross sacked the city and murdered thousands of its people. One of the crusades was actually led by a 12-year-old boy. More than 20,000 children died in this crusade.

Crusader castles dot the coast of Israel. Remains of the Crusades period can be seen in Acco, Caesarea, and Hebron.

Godfrey of Bouillon one of the leaders of the First Crusade (1096), leaves for the Holy Land.

This painting shows the crusaders besieging Jerusalem. The giant catapult was able to throw a 100-pound stone into the city.

Hospitaller   Teutonic Knight   Templar

The crusaders were led by groups called military orders. Each order represented a different segment of the Christian religion.

The Knights Hospitaller were guardians of the Hospital of St. John in Jerusalem. The Knights Templar guarded the palace of the king of Jerusalem. The Teutonic knights were of German origin.

Belvoir Castle was built by the French Knights Hospitaller. It was destroyed in the thirteenth century by the sultan of Damascus, who was afraid that the crusaders would return. The stone arches are a part of the ruins of Belvoir.

A page from a French history book written in 1337. The painting shows the crusader attack on Jerusalem.

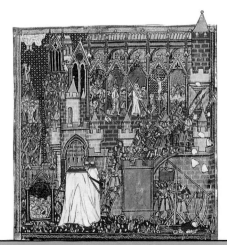

Crusaders storming the walls of Jerusalem. From a fifteenth-century French manuscript.

The First Aliyah

The Hebrew word *aliyah* means "going up."

In Temple days Jews made aliyah by ascending the hills of Judea and climbing the steps of the Holy Temple to offer a sacrifice. The word aliyah also refers to the "going up" to the reader's desk in the synagogue to take part in the Torah service.

Returning to Zion is also designated by the term aliyah. It too is a form of "going up," for in returning to Zion one ascends from life in exile to the proud Land of Israel. Each Jew who settles in Israel receives the honored title of *oleh* (for a man or boy) or *olah* (for a woman or girl), which means, "one who goes up" or "makes aliyah." The plural form is *olim*.

As the nineteenth century drew to a close, European Jews were shocked and frightened by the pogroms sweeping Russia. Mobs killed thousands of innocent Jewish people. Many were inspired by the passionate speeches of Theodor Herzl, calling upon them to settle in Palestine.

Between 1882 and 1904, in what is known as the First Aliyah, 25,000 olim moved to the Land of Israel. They joined the 25,000 Jews already living in the four holy cities—Jerusalem, Hebron, Tiberias, and Safed.

During the First Aliyah the first farming settlements—Petach Tikvah, Rishon Le-Zion, Rosh Pinah, and Zichron Yaakov—were formed. The developing Jewish community of Palestine was known as the Yishuv. Its new settlements were helped by Baron Edmond de Rothschild. He supported them financially and sent experts to help them with their agricul-

tural problems.

Under the leadership of Eliezer Ben-Yehuda the Hebrew language was modernized and revised. Within ten years Hebrew had become the principal language of the Yishuv.

One of the first groups of Jewish watchmen (1904) in the Galilee. Israel Shohat, Hashomer's first commander, is in the center of the photo.

A Jewish farm family in Rishon Le-Zion reaps the grape harvest. Note the leaf-covered watchtower. During the harvest season, armed Jewish watchmen protected the crops from Arab raiders.

The leafy hut on stilts is a sukkah. Ancient Jewish farmers, also standing guard to protect their crops from raiders, built sukkot to shade themselves from the hot sun.

Baron Edmond de Rothschild

The family name Rothschild comes from two German words, *roth*, meaning "red," and *schild*, meaning "shield." A red shield identified the house of Isaac Elhanan, the founder of the Rothschild family in Frankfurt, Germany, in the seventeenth century.

Mayer Amschel Rothschild, a descendant of Isaac Elhanan, was a banker. His five sons established branch banks in five major European capitals: Frankfurt, Paris, Vienna, Naples, and London. Wherever the Rothschilds settled, they used their wealth and economic power to help their fellow Jews.

The first farm settlements in Israel were founded during the First Aliyah. The first four settlements were Petach Tikvah, Rishon Le-Zion, Rosh Pinah, and Zichron Yaakov. The first settlers were from the cities of Europe and knew very little about farming. To add to their troubles, they found a dry, rocky, barren land infested with malaria. The difficulties of the farmers made the existence of the settlements very much in doubt.

Shortly after the first settlements were founded, the Ottoman authorities banned all further Jewish immigration and settlement, which now had to be carried on illegally.

As a last resort, the desperate settlers sent an emissary to Baron Edmond de Rothschild of Paris, asking for help. Disaster was averted by the baron, who came to be known as the Father of the Yishuv.

He took the villages and the settlements under his wing and provided money and agricultural experts. In addition, he managed to purchase 125,000 acres of

Baron Edmond de Rothschild

land from the Ottomans for additional farms and settlements.

The expulsion of Jews from Moscow in 1891 led to a new wave of legal and illegal immigration into the homeland.

The baron's agricultural experts taught the settlers how to plant a variety of crops. He was instrumental in starting the wine industry in the Land of Israel. His company purchased all the grapes which the settlers produced at a higher than market price.

There are now 21 wineries in Israel located in every section of the country.

Today the Carmel operation, started by the baron, is a cooperative marketing enterprise embracing among its partners kibbutzim, moshavim, and private vineyards. Carmel possesses 70 percent of the Israeli market and exports its wine throughout the world.

Baron Rothschild also found time to fund the Hebrew University in Jerusalem. In his lifetime the Father of the Yishuv provided more money for the homeland than all the Jews in the world combined.

The Rothschild family has continued its support for the State of Israel. There are numerous schools, hospitals, parks, and museums funded by this generous Jewish family.

Joseph Trumpeldor

Joseph Trumpeldor (1880–1920) was an inspirational model for the Zionist pioneers.

During his youth in Russia, Joseph Trumpeldor became a Zionist and dreamed of settling in Israel. He was drafted into the Russian army and lost an arm while fighting in the Russo-Japanese War.

Despite his handicap, Trumpeldor went to Eretz Yisrael, where he lived and worked at Degania. He used his experience in the Russian army to organize defenses for the new Jewish settlements.

During World War I he helped Vladimir Jabotinsky form the Zion Mule Corps, which fought with the British armed forces. He later became an officer in the Jewish Legion, the volunteer army which defended the settlements in Palestine.

The Jewish Legion was an army of volunteers from countries all over the world. Jewish Legion soldiers proudly wore the Magen David on their uniforms, spoke Hebrew, and saluted the Zionist flag as well as the British flag.

The Jewish Legion consisted of 2,700 volunteers from the United States, South Africa, Russia, Argentina, and Mexico. Among the recruits in the Jewish Legion

Joseph Trumpeldor was an officer in the Russian army. He lost an arm fighting in the Russo-Japanese War. In this photo he is wearing his Russian uniform and the medals that he won for bravery in action.

was David Green, a young Jewish immigrant from Russia. As David Ben-Gurion, Green became the first Prime Minister of Israel.

After World War I the Arabs began attacking the Jewish settlements in the Galilee. One-armed Joseph Trumpeldor led the defense of Kibbutz Tel Hai. Eight settlers, including Trumpeldor, were killed by Arab raiders. The dying words of this Jewish hero reveal his love of Israel: "It is good to die for our country."

A youth group was named in his honor: Betar, short for B'rith Trumpeldor, "The Covenant of Trumpeldor."

In Israel, the 11th day of the month of Adar is Tel Hai Day. Many Israelis make a pilgrimage to the cemetery of Tel Hai to honor the memory of Joseph Trumpeldor and the other heroes who died defending the homeland.

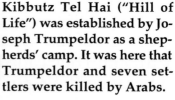

Kibbutz Tel Hai ("Hill of Life") was established by Joseph Trumpeldor as a shepherds' camp. It was here that Trumpeldor and seven settlers were killed by Arabs.

The Balfour Declaration

Chaim Weizmann (1874-1952) was a brilliant chemist. During World War I the British were in desperate need of acetone for the manufacture of explosives. They entrusted Weizmann with this important task and he quickly synthesized the needed chemical. The British were thankful and wished to award him for his services. However, he asked nothing for himself, only something for the homeland of the Jewish people. In appreciation for his services the British issued the famous Balfour Declaration.

Lord Arthur James Balfour was a leader of England's Conservative Party. During his tenure as Foreign Secretary he wrote to Baron Rothschild on November 2, 1917 that "His Majesty's government view with favor the establishment in Palestine of a national home for the Jewish people, and will use their best endeavors to facilitate the achievement of this object." He promised that Britain would exert every effort to gain that end, but that nothing would be done to injure the rights of the non-Jews in Palestine.

The Balfour Declaration was endorsed by France, Italy, Japan, and the United States. It became part of the League of Nations document that gave Great Britain its Mandate over Palestine. The Mandate gave Britain temporary control of Palestine until the people were capable of ruling themselves.

Despite the Balfour Declaration, the British government refused to honor its pledge. Britain used a "divide and rule" concept to administer the Mandate. It played Jew against Arab to aggravate the political situation.

During the thirty years of their Mandate over Palestine, the British obstructed the return of Jewish refugees from the lands of persecution. Jews from Russia and Poland were not allowed to enter the country legally. Especially vicious was the denial of entry to Jews from the lands of the Holocaust—from Germany, Austria, and Poland, to name a few.

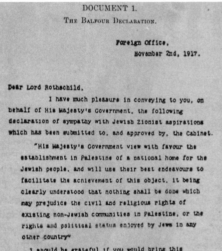

The Balfour Declaration.

Lord Arthur James Balfour

The Third Aliyah

The Third Aliyah (1919–1923) was spearheaded by young members of the Hechalutz movement in Russia and Poland who joined hands with the pioneers of the Second Aliyah.

Forty thousand more olim reached Israel in the years between 1919 and 1923. They believed in the same goals as the previous Zionist settlers—working and sharing, social justice, self-defense, and speaking Hebrew. The new wave of pioneers endured great hardships, but they persisted in the work of rebuilding Israel. Many new kibbutzim were established. Hebrew literature, journalism, and theater came into being.

The Haganah began in 1920 and was Israel's first military defense organization. Haganah members protected major cities in Israel as well as moshavim and kibbutzim. Despite the restrictions and the difficult living conditions, there were more than 80,000 Jews in the land.

Arab nationalist leaders demanded an end to Jewish immigration and the establishment of an independent Arab state.

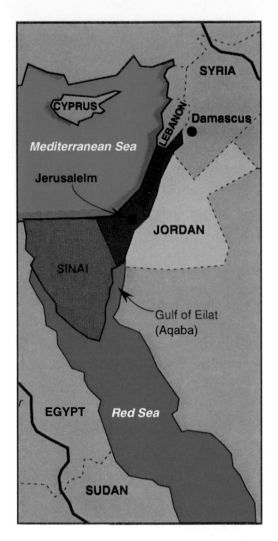

The British government, in 1922, divided the promised Jewish homeland by cutting off three-quarters of the land area of Palestine. A new Arab state was created, called Transjordan. In 1946 Transjordan became independent. It is now called Jordan.

Lawrence of Arabia arranged a meeting between Emir Feisal and Chaim Weizmann. Dr. Weizmann travelled by boat and by camel to discuss the Palestinian situation with the emir. These two intelligent leaders developed a friendship and respect for each other's views.

The Emir and Dr. Weizmann issued a statement agreeing to the recognition of Zionist aims in Palestine if the Arabs were given independence in Syria and Iraq. The territories, which were then ruled by the French and the British, were not given independence and the Jewish-Arab alliance collapsed.

The Fourth Aliyah

The Fourth Aliyah (1924–1928) brought shopkeepers and artisans, mostly from Poland, where anti-Semitic restrictions were being applied. The majority of the new arrivals settled in the cities of Tel Aviv, Haifa, and Jerusalem.

Many of the newcomers had difficulty adapting to their new environment. However in 1928 the economic climate began to improve.

Pincus Rutenberg harnessed the waters of the Jordan River and built a power station which provided electricity for new farms and factories. Business, industry and farming absorbed the growing labor force.

Progress was rapid on many other levels. The Jewish National Council (Vaad Leumi) organized an educational system that covered the entire Yishuv on every level from preschool to university. In 1925, the Hebrew University in Jerusalem was officially opened. The city of Tel Aviv was rapidly expanding and developing into the nerve center of the newly immerging nation.

During the years 1924 to 1928 some 90,000 additional Jews came to Israel. At the end of this period the Jewish population of Israel reached about 170,000.

Pincus Rutenberg, an engineer and Zionist leader, founded the Palestine Electric Company in 1931. He built a hydro-electric generating plant at the point where the Yarmuk and Jordan rivers meet. The dam channeled the waters into the plant, which turned the turbines and generated electricity.

The Hebrew University was first founded on Mount Scopus in Jerusalem in 1925.
The first books for the library were brought by a donkey.

Alexander Zeid (1886–1938)
He was a pioneer of the Second Aliyah and one of the founders of the Hashomer. He was killed by Arabs while on guard duty in 1938. A statue of Zeid on horseback was erected in the settlement of Givat Zeid, named in his honor. This Israeli stamp features the statue of Alexander Zeid.

Henrietta Szold

Henrietta Szold

Henrietta Szold (1860–1945) is known as the Mother of Israel. She never married, but she had 50,000 children.

Henrietta Szold was born in Baltimore, Maryland. Her rabbi father made sure that she received an excellent Jewish education. After high school graduation, she became a teacher of Hebrew, Bible, and Jewish history.

In 1909 she visited Israel and was appalled by the misery and disease of the Zionist settlers. When she returned to the United States, Henrietta decided to help the settlers. Together with some friends she formed a new group which called itself Hadassah, and Henrietta became its first president in 1914. The women who joined it raised money to improve the health conditions of Jews and Arabs in Israel. Branches of this organization grew up all over the United States.

After World War I, at the age of 60, Henrietta Szold moved to Israel so she could be on the scene to organize and direct the efforts of Hadassah. One of its most important achievements was the building of a modern hospital on Mount Scopus in Jerusalem.

In 1932 she founded Youth Aliyah. The aim was to save the Jewish children of Europe from the impending Holocaust. By the end of World War II more than 50,000 children had been rescued. When they arrived in Israel they were taken in by families who shared their homes and their love with them. Henrietta Szold also helped form special Youth Aliyah villages to house some of the young refugees.

In 1945, at the age of 85, Henrietta died. At her funeral a 15-year-old orphan boy stood at her graveside and recited the Kaddish.

She had no children of her own, but the 50,000 Youth Aliyah children called her "Mamma."

After her death, a fund that she had started for youth activities was named Mosad Szold (Szold Foundation).

Aerial view of the Hadassah Medical Center on Mount Scopus in Jerusalem.

Hannah Senesh

Hannah Senesh was born in Hungary in 1921 and as a young child revealed a special literary talent. In 1939, Hungarian anti-Semitism induced her to leave her family and emigrate to Israel. Hannah began her agricultural studies at Nahalal, a moshav. Two years later she joined Kibbutz S'dot Yam, near Caesarea. At the kibbutz she managed to find time to continue her literary career and wrote many poems.

In the meantime, the Nazis gained strength and occupied most of Europe. Death camps were built and whole Jewish communities were wiped out. The "Final Solution" was in progress.

In 1942 Hannah Senesh joined the Haganah and volunteered to return to Hungary to organize and arm Jewish resistance movements against the Nazis. Hannah parachuted into Yugoslavia, where she joined General Tito's anti-Nazi guerrilla fighters. A German spy among the guerrillas informed the Nazis about Hannah's plans. Her disguise did not fool the Hungarian police, and she was arrested at a border crossing.

The Nazis tortured her, but Hannah refused to reveal any information about the Jewish underground. On November 7, 1944, Hannah Senesh, a 24-year-old Jewish heroine, was executed by a Hungarian firing squad.

After the war her body was recovered and returned to her beloved homeland of Israel. Hannah is buried on Mount Herzl among the thousands of brave heroes and heroines who gave their lives for freedom.

The passport of Hannah Senesh

Hannah Senesh wrote this short letter before she parachuted into Yugloslavia. The letter reads,

"My friends of Kibbutz Caesarea,
By sea, by land, in war and in peace,
we are all marching for one purpose.
Each one must do their duty. I will
keep all of you in my memory. This
will give me strength.

Warm best wishes.

    Hannah"

The War of Independence

Despite Arab protests, the United Nations, on November 29, 1947, passed a resolution in favor of partitioning Palestine into two parts, one Arab and one Jewish. Seven months later, on May 14, 1948, the British gave up the Mandate and left Palestine. The Jews immediately set up their own government under the leadership of David Ben-Gurion.

The very next day, the armies of Egypt, Syria, Jordan, Lebanon, and Saudi Arabia invaded the newborn State of Israel. Masses of Arab tanks supported by bomber planes assaulted Jewish settlements. Haganah-trained men, women, and children resisted the invaders. Survivors of the concentration camps fought side by side with veteran settlers. Arms and ammunition were in short supply, yet spirits and morale remained high.

The Israelis held out against ferocious attacks by Arab artillery, armored cars, and aircraft. On isolated kibbutzim in the Galilee and the Negev, the settlers defended themselves with rifles, mortars, and homemade Molotov cocktails.

In January 1949, after months of fighting and thousands of casualties on both sides, a truce was declared. Twenty months after the first attack, the severely beaten Arab governments agreed to end the war.

Israel's stunning victory came at great human cost. More than 4,000 of the finest and bravest soldiers and 3,000 civilians lost their lives defending the homeland.

The yearning of so many Jews, during the 2,000 years of exile, was now realized. Israel was reborn! The Jews now had a homeland of their own.

Mordecai Anielewicz helped organize the revolt against the Nazis in the Warsaw Ghetto. He died fighting the Germans. This statue in memory of Mordecai Anielewicz is at Kibbutz Yad Mordecai in Israel.

Women played an important role in the War of Independence. They were an essential part of many combat teams.

THE PALESTINE POST

If you can't come to town, please telephone 4607

Lighting, Heating, Cooking, Refrigeration

2 PRINCESS MARY AVE, JERUSALEM

JERUSALEM SUNDAY, MAY 16, 1948

PRICE: 25 MILS VOL. XXIII. No. 6714

THE PALESTINE POST

THE SUBSCRIPTION DEPARTMENT has returned to The Palestine Post offices, Hasolel Street, Jerusalem, Tel. 4233.

STATE OF ISRAEL IS BORN

The first independent Jewish State in nineteen centuries was born in Tel Aviv as the British Mandate over Palestine came to an end at midnight on Friday, and it was immediately subjected to the test of fire. A "Medinat Yisrael" (State of Israel) was proclaimed, the battle for Jerusalem raged, with most of the city falling to the Jews. At the same time, President Truman announced that the United States would accord recognition to the new State. A few hours later, Palestine was invaded by Moslem armies from the south, east and north, and Tel Aviv was raided from the air. On Friday the United Nations Special assembly adjourned after adopting a resolution to appoint a mediator but without taking any action on the Partition Resolution of November 29. Yesterday the battle for the Jerusalem–Tel Aviv road was still under way, and two Arab villages were taken. In the north, Acre town was captured, and the Jewish Army consolidated its positions in Western Galilee.

U.S. RECOGNIZES JEWISH STATE

Washington, Saturday. Ten minutes after the termination of the British Mandate on Friday, the White House released a formal statement by President Truman that the U.S. Government intended to recognize the Provisional Jewish Government as the de facto authority representing the Jewish State.

The U.S. is also considering lifting the arms embargo but it is not known whether to Palestine only or the entire Middle East, and the establishment of diplomatic relations with the Jewish Provisional government.

In Frankfurt, General Lucius D. Clay, the U.S. Military Commander of Germany, said today that Jews in Germany and Austria would be assisted to leave for the State of Israel as soon as official word of America's recognition was announced.

ACRE CAPTURED

Acre, the sea-coast town across the bay from Haifa, was captured by Jewish forces yesterday, the Haganah Radio reported. The surrender of the town, and subsequently two villages to the north came after a strong Jewish attack.

Armed camps containing enormous quantites of military equipment were captured.

PROCLAMATION OF MEDINAT YISRAEL

The creation of "Medinat Ysrael" the State of Israel, was proclaimed at midnight on Friday, by Mr. David Ben Gurion, until then Chairman of the Jewish Agency Executive and now head of the State's Provisional Council of Government.

The first act of the Council of Government, as announced by its head, was to abolish all legislation of the 1939 White Paper of the late Mandatory Power, particularly the Ordinances and Orders relating to immigration and land transfer.

In the declaration of independence, Mr. Ben Gurion called on the Arabs of Palestine to restore peace, assuring them full civic rights and full representation in all governmental organs of the State.

The Balfour Declaration of 1917, confirmed by the League of Nations, had given explicit international recognition to the right of the Jewish people to reconstitute its National Home in Palestine, he said.

"On November 29, 1947," continued the declaration "the United Nations decided on the establishment of a Jewish State and an Arab state in Palestine and called upon the inhabitants of the country to take all steps necessary for the establishment of the two States.

RUSSIAN RECOGNITION AWAITED

Russia and her allies had given early assurance of their intention to recognize the Jewish State, whoever else did or did not. As a result of Washington's action and the Eastern Bloc's stand, other countries are expected to extend their recognition to the newly born state.

2 VILLAGES TAKEN

In the battle for the Tel Aviv Jerusalem road, the Haganah on Friday night took Kubeib and Abu Shusha villages between Latrun and Ramle. In engagements elsewhere along the route positions near Latrun and Bab el Wad changed hands.

Jewish casualties in this area in the last two days are about 40 killed. the Iraqis suffered greater losses, but their exact number is unknown.

The Suez Campaign

The War of Independence in 1948 was followed by a short period of quiet. For Israel it was the best of times; for eight years there was no large-scale shooting war. For Israel it was the worst of times. For eight years there was a war of threats and terrorist attacks against the infant state.

In 1956, President Gamal Abdul Nasser of Egypt decided to close the Suez Canal to Israeli shipping and ships trading with Israel. The Arabs were now applying pressure against Israel on all sides, slowly choking Israel's economy. Israel needed to keep open its shipping lanes, its lifeline to the outside world.

The Suez Canal is a waterway in Egypt connecting the Mediterranean and the Red Sea. It was planned and built by the French in 1859. In 1875, the British became its largest stockholder. Under the terms of the treaty signed at that time, Egypt was to take complete control in 1968, but Nasser was unwilling to wait. Egypt's seizure of the canal endangered the British and French economies and their political position in the Middle East.

On October 29, 1956, Israeli, French, and British forces launched a combined attack against Egypt. In an eight-day campaign, Israeli forces, under the command of General Moshe Dayan, captured the Gaza Strip and the entire Sinai Peninsula. IDF ground and motorized troops barreled their way to the Suez Canal. The combined British and French forces managed to capture parts of the Suez Canal.

At this point the United States and Russia stepped in, forcing the British and French to withdraw from the Canal and allow Egypt complete control. Israel refused to withdraw from its position on the Suez Canal until a United Nations peacekeeping force was placed along the Egypt-Israel border. As part of the settlement the United Nations guaranteed that Israeli shipping would have complete access to the Suez Canal.

With this guarantee, Israel was now in a position to develop trading links with the Asian and African countries. It also now had an open port, Eilat, for importing oil from the Persian Gulf.

Israeli soldiers shout in triumph as they reach the Suez Canal.

An Israeli armored column waiting its turn to cross the Suez Canal.

Eichmann the Butcher

Jews have long memories, and sometimes many years go by before a wrong against them is avenged. After World War II many of the monsters who murdered Jews during the Holocaust escaped. Some found safe haven in Arab countries. Many escaped to South America, where they lived under new identities. In many instances they were protected by anti-Semitic government officials.

Israel organized a special group of secret Nazi hunters whose job it was to find and expose these criminals.

In 1941, Adolf Otto Eichmann had been placed in charge of the Jews in the concentration camps. He was the head of the Department of Jewish Affairs at Nazi headquarters in Berlin. Eichmann organized the deportation of Jews to the death camps and was responsible for stealing their property.

Eichmann on trial in Israel.

After the war he was captured by the Allies, but in 1950 he managed to escape to Argentina. Officials in the government furnished him with false identification papers, and he lived there till 1960, when he was discovered by the Israeli Nazi hunters. Eichmann was kidnapped and secretly flown to Israel to stand trial. After a long trial he was found guilty and sentenced to death. His body was cremated, just as he had cremated six million Jews, and his ashes were scattered over the Mediterranean Sea.

His was the first and only execution ever carried out by the State of Israel.

Memorial to the Warsaw Ghetto Uprising at Yad Vashem.

The Haganah

In the early 1900s, during the First and Second Aliyot, there were numerous attacks against Jewish settlements in Eretz Yisrael. Hundreds of Jews were murdered and much property was destroyed.

The Talmud states, "Rise up and defeat those who come to murder you." In response to these attacks, the Jews "rose up" and established a tiny defense force called Hashomer ("The Watchman").

Hashomer had only 100 members. But each shomer was a deadly marksman, an expert horseman, and was fluent in Arabic.

In 1920, Hashomer was disbanded and a more powerful group called Haganah ("The Defense") was established. Heavily armed Haganah members, male and female, actively defended the Jews in the cities and in the settlements.

During the Arab riots of 1929, Haganah volunteers saved the Jewish communities of Jerusalem, Tel Aviv, and Haifa from mass destruction. After 1929 the Haganah began a period of expansion and improved training by professional soldiers. Modern arms were smuggled into Palestine in barrels of cement and agricultural machinery crates.

By 1939, the Haganah had 25,000 highly trained members armed with smuggled rifles, machine guns, and homemade grenades manufactured in secret factories. During World War II, the Haganah expanded its role by parachuting spies into Nazi-occupied territory to organize armed resistance against the enemy. At the same time, hundreds of Haganah members joined the Jewish Brigade of the British army. The Brigade fought bravely in Egypt and in Italy.

After the war, the British continued their pro-Arab policy of restricting Jewish immigration into Eretz Yisrael. The Haganah countered by destroying British radar stations, bridges, and other military establishments. The Haganah's main activity during the period of 1945–1948 was the organization of illegal immigration into Palestine. Tens of thousands of so-called "illegal immigrants" were smuggled into the country.

On May 15, 1948, when the State of Israel was established, the Haganah faced the regular armies of the surrounding Arab states. The British, as usual, helped the Arabs by handing them key military positions and fortifications. Despite the British actions and the superior numbers of the Arab forces, the Haganah managed to repel the enemy attacks. On May 31, 1948 the Haganah officially became Tzahal, the regular army of Israel.

This photo was taken at Kibbutz Hanita in 1938. *Left to right:* Moshe Dayan, Yitzchak Sadeh, and Yigal Allon. Each of these young men became a high-ranking officer in the Haganah as well as an important political leader.

Diplomats and Spies

The State of Israel has diplomatic relations with most of the countries of the world. Only the Arab states and a few African and Asian countries still do not recognize Israel.

When two countries have diplomatic relations, they exchange ambassadors. Thus Israel has ambassadors in many countries. The ambassador represents Israel and protects its citizens in the country where he or she is assigned. This includes helping them with lost passports and assisting them when they are in trouble.

Another duty of Israel's ambassadors and diplomats is to meet important political, military, and business leaders of that country. In this way they promote trade and explain Israeli policies and problems.

Diplomats also try to obtain information about the government's political policy and its military plans concerning Israel and the Middle East.

Unfriendly countries do not cooperate and share information with Israel. So Israel resorts to other means of gathering information, such as spying and satellites.

Israel has satellites that fly over enemy countries and photograph troop movements, military air fields, and army camps.

Spying is another way of getting information about a country. The Mosad is in charge of training spies and assembling information about enemy countries.

Eli Cohen was Israel's most famous spy. He was born in Egypt, where he learned the Arabic language and Arab customs. Later he moved to Israel and was trained as a spy. The Mosad sent him to Syria, where he used an Arabic name and pretended to be a rich Syrian citizen. He spoke the language so well that no one guessed he was really an Israeli.

Cohen became friendly with military officers who told him important secrets. He was taken on tours of secret army bases and air fields.

This secret part fit so well that he began his own show on Syrian radio. He was a well-known personality throughout the Syrian nation.

In 1964 Eli Cohen was discovered by Russian intelligence and sentenced to be hanged. The hanging was televised throughout the Arab world. Arabs cheered, but Israelis mourned the loss of a brave patriot who had given his life for his country.

Eli Cohen, Israeli master spy.

The Yom Kippur War

Almost daily between 1968 and 1970, marauding Arab terrorists sneaked across Israel's borders to attack innocent people. Tel Aviv was shelled. A school bus was blown up in Eilat injuring 28 children. The Arab leaders ignored their promises of peace and encouraged their people to hate the Jewish state. Russia encouraged the Arabs and sent them billions of dollars worth of arms.

On October 6, 1973—the holy day of Yom Kippur—the Arabs attacked Israel on two fronts at once. Syria attacked Israel's northern Golan front, and Egypt attacked across the Suez Canal into the Sinai.

Since Yom Kippur is the most sacred day of the Jewish year, most soldiers were in the synagogues with their families. The Arab sneak attack succeeded and caught Israel off guard.

By the time Israel's troops could assemble to defend their land, the invading Arab armies had broken through the Israeli lines to both the north and the south. Massive Egyptian and Syrian armies penetrated the Israeli defenses, the Egyptians pushing into Sinai and the Syrians moving into the Golan Heights.

By the third day, Israel recovered fast and started to take the offensive. With prayerbooks in one hand and machine guns in the other, Israeli soldiers left the synagogues and went straight to the battlefield. In nine days the Israeli army pushed back all the invaders. The Egyptian army was surrounded in the Sinai and Israeli troops threatened Cairo, Egypt's capital. The Syrians also had been forced back. Israel was poised to attack Damascus, Syria's capital.

Now that Israel was winning, the Arabs and the Russians went to the United Nations and pleaded for help.

The Jewish nation wanted peace, not bloodshed. And so Israel agreed to a ceasefire despite its position of strength at this point in the war. On October 24, just 18 days after the Arab invasion, the fighting stopped.

After the ceasefire, all of Israel mourned the nation's loss of its finest soldiers. Golda Meir, the Prime Minister, said: "For the people of Israel, each human life is precious. Our dead soldiers are the sons of all of us. The pain we feel is felt by all of us."

As a result of the surprise attack, Prime Minister Golda Meir was forced to resign. Many voters had lost confidence in her ruling Labor Party. Yitzchak Rabin, of the Labor Party, became the new Prime Minister.

But the Arabs did not speak of peace. Even after signing the ceasefire agreement, Egypt and Syria pretended they had won the war.

An Arab poster depicts Israel as a snake. An Arab knife is severing its head from its body.

The Israel-Egypt Peace Treaty

In May 1977, a new government was elected in Israel. The Likud Party, headed by Menachem Begin, became the largest party in the Knesset.

The new Prime Minister invited President Sadat of Egypt to come to Jerusalem. Menachem Begin wanted peace for Israel, and he hoped that through a talk with the Arab leader, peace with Egypt might be reached. In November 1977, for the first time ever, an Arab leader, President Anwar Sadat of Egypt, visited Jerusalem. Sadat spoke in the Knesset of his wish for peace between Egypt and Israel. The Jews hoped and prayed that Sadat's visit would begin a new era of peace and understanding. But many found it difficult to trust Egypt's promises. The Arab nations had never lived up to their promises of peace before.

On March 26, 1979, a peace treaty was signed between Israel and Egypt in Washington, D.C. Prime Minister Menachem Begin of Israel, President Anwar Sadat of Egypt, and President Jimmy Carter of the United States worked hard to bring about the signing of this historic agreement. It is called the Camp David Agreement, from the name of the place where the three leaders met with each other.

The other Arab states bitterly opposed Sadat's steps toward peace with Israel. They swore to have their revenge on him for having negotiated with the Jewish state. In October 1981, Sadat was killed by an assassin's bullet.

Begin, Carter and Sadat after the peace treaty was signed in Washington on March 26, 1979.

Rescue at Entebbe

Lieutenant Colonel Yonathan Netanyahu.

The C-130 Hercules transport plane in which the Israel commando forces were flown to Entebbe.

Wars are fought on many different levels. There are battlefields where soldiers, tanks, and airplanes shoot at each other. But there is also war by terrorism directed against innocent civilians. Bombs are planted in department stores, civilians are shot or stabbed on the street, explosives are planted in automobiles.

On June 27, 1976 an Air France plane carrying 300 people was hijacked by terrorists.

The plane with its 300 men, women, and children was forced to land at Entebbe, the capital of the African nation of Uganda. The terrorists demanded that Israel release terrorists being held in Israeli jails in exchange for the passengers.

This hijacking took place with the cooperation of the Ugandan government, headed by Idi Amin. He was known as the butcher of Uganda because of his savage cruelty. All non-Jewish prisoners were released, but more than 100 Jews were kept and threatened with death.

Israel did not wait for the U.N. or any country to help. The Israel Defense Forces set up a plan called Operation Yonathan, named for its leader, Col. Yonathan (Yoni) Netanyahu.

At a very young age Yoni Netanyahu had distinguished himself as an officer with the paratroopers. In 1967 he fought in the Six-Day War and was wounded. In 1973 he fought bravely in the Yom Kippur War. Now Yoni was entrusted with the job of freeing the Jewish prisoners in Entebbe.

Under cover of darkness, transport planes carried 100 highly trained Israeli commandos to Entebbe, more than 2,500 miles from Israel. The unmarked planes flew an indirect course to avoid detection.

The Israeli troops silently deplaned and in a short fight quickly eliminated the Ugandan troops and the terrorists.

Within 90 minutes the hostages were on the plane and on the way back to safety.

There was one tragic death. Col. Yoni Netanyahu, the leader of the raiding party, was killed. His death was mourned by Jews all over the world.

Several months later Idi Amin, the butcher of Uganda, was overthrown. He found refuge in Saudi Arabia.

Mission to Iraq

For more than 30 years the Middle Eastern countries have had the pick of world weaponry—short of nuclear arms. In 1980 the Israeli government grew very anxious over the growth of Iraqi military power, especially in the area of nuclear, chemical and biological weapons. Israel was especially concerned about the nuclear production facilities in the Iraqi city of Osirak, which French, German, and British scientists were building 10 miles from Bagdad.

On June 7, 1981 Israeli fighter-bombers attacked the factory. Eight Israeli bombers, escorted by fighter planes, flew about 600 miles through enemy air space and dropped sixteen 2,000-lb. bombs on the nuclear facility. The factory was destroyed and all the aircraft returned safely.

The whole world condemned Israel, but secretly most of Iraq's neighbors applauded the raid.

There have been continual efforts by Iraq to produce nuclear, chemical, biological, and neurological weapons. Reliable sources report that the Iraqis have killed more than 50,000 men, women and children with these weapons in their wars against Iran and the Kurds. Many U.S. soldiers who served in the Gulf War against Iraq have complained of mysterious diseases for which doctors can find no causes or cures. Some military sources claim that Iraq used biological weapons during the war.

After the Gulf War in 1993, U.N. inspectors identified numerous Iraqi nuclear and poison gas facilities.

What would have happened to the soldiers of the military coalition in the Gulf War if Israel had not destroyed Iraq's nuclear capabilities in 1981?

To this day no one has given Israel credit for saving the world from a nuclear Holocaust by a power-hungry dictator.

Saddam Hussein, President of Iraq, launched an ambitious program to modernize his arsenal of offensive weapons. He built chemical, gas and biological weapons and used them against the Kurds and Iranians. In addition he began building a nuclear weapons facility at Osirak. In 1981 an Israeli air attack destroyed the half-built reactor.

Peace for Galilee

Lebanon is an independent country bordered by both Israel and Syria. Its population is almost evenly divided between Muslims and Maronite Christians. A parliamentary government divides the official positions evenly between the two religious groups.

Before 1970, Lebanon was a very prosperous and modern country with a highly skilled and educated work force. It was the banking and trading center of the Middle East. Lebanon was also a pipeline center for oil coming from Saudi Arabia and Iraq.

Beirut, the capital of Lebanon, was the play center of the Middle East. Its night-clubs and gambling palaces were in constant 24-hour motion. Arab sheiks, millionaires, and government officials made frequent trips to sample its rich and luxurious lifestyle that is forbidden by the Koran.

In 1970 the PLO was expelled by Jordan and set up shop in Lebanon. Israeli settlements along the Lebanese border now came under frequent attack by shells, rockets, and artillery. Jews in the border towns and in the Galilee had to live in shelters to protect themselves from PLO bombardments.

Beginning in 1975, a brutal civil war was fought between the Christians and the Arabs. After many battles and thousands of casualties, the Syrians moved in and restored order. They became the muscle behind a new Lebanese government. The Syrians allowed the PLO to continue the attacks on northern Israel.

On July 6, 1982, the IDF launched Operation Peace for Galilee. The Israeli army, under the command of General Ariel Sharon, dashed into Lebanon and captured the city of Beirut. Many of the PLO terrorists and their Syrian allies were killed or captured. A large amount of guns, tanks, and missiles were also taken.

Most Lebanese Christians were happy to see the Israelis. They had been robbed and beaten by the PLO and the Syrian troops. Now, thanks to the Israelis, they once again had their freedom.

Prime Minister Menachem Begin hoped that the PLO threat would be ended once and for all. But Operation Peace for Galilee caused much controversy. Thousands of Israelis protested against the military actions of the Likud government.

In 1983 most of the IDF was recalled and Prime Minister Begin resigned.

A small contingent of Israeli troops and Christian Lebanese militia still maintained a small security zone on the frontier to prevent terrorist infiltration into Israel. Despite the troops there are still enemy incursions and rocket attacks

General Ariel Sharon commanded Operation Peace for Galilee.

Israel and the Gulf War

In July 1990 President Saddam Hussein, of Iraq threatened to use force against any Arab country that continued to pump oil above its OPEC quota. The price of a barrel of oil had fallen from $20 to $13. Each dollar dropped meant a $1 billion loss for Iraqi oil revenue. This threat was especially aimed at the kingdom of Kuwait, which was exporting oil above its OPEC quota.

On August 2, 1990, 100,000 Iraqi troops invaded Kuwait and quickly took control of the country. Six hundred oil wells were set afire. Torture, killings, mass arrests, and stealing of anything of value continued without a stop. The whole world condemned the invasion except King Hussein of Jordan and the PLO.

On August 7, 1990 President George Bush set in motion Operation Desert Storm under the command of General Norman Schwarzkoff. A huge airlift of soldiers, arms and ammunition began flowing into staging areas in Saudi Arabia.

Israel was not in the coalition forces because the Arab members, notably Saudi Arabia, Egypt and Kuwait, did not want to be seen fighting side-by-side with Israel against their Arab brothers. President Bush pressured a promise from Yitzchak Shamir, Prime Minister of Israel, not to initiate a strike against Iraqi Scud missile installations.

At the start of the war Israel distributed gas masks to all of its citizens; Jewish, Muslim and Christian. Iraqi threats to use poison gas were no idle boast. They had already gassed 50,000 Iraqis and Kurds.

On the first night of the war, eight Scud missiles hit Israel, two in Haifa, two in Tel Aviv and four in unpopulated areas. As the missiles fell, Arabs in the West Bank were seen cheering on the rooftops.

Saddam Hussein fired a total of 86 Scud missiles, 40 at Israel and 46 at Saudi Arabia. Some were blown up by United States Patriot missiles. In Israel 250 people were wounded. In and around Tel Aviv about 9,000 apartments were damaged. The most lethal Scud attack was on barracks in Saudi Arabia filled with U.S. troops. Twenty-eight Americans were killed.

The U.S. was aware that the Israeli air force had targeted Iraqi mobile and static missile sites. To deter Israel's response, President Bush sent two Patriot missile batteries to Israel to shoot down the incoming Scud missiles. The Patriot missiles succeeded. Only one Scud landed in Tel Aviv and caused much property damage.

The ground combat phase of the Gulf War lasted a little more than 100 hours. The Iraqi army was easily destroyed by a combination of tanks, artillery and air power. To this day no one has calculated the number of Iraqis who lost their lives in this senseless war.

As a consequence of Iraq's defeat the power balance in the Middle East shifted. The PLO lost its financial backers, Saudi Arabia and Kuwait, because it supported Saddam Hussein. This shift made it possible for Israel to reach an agreement with the PLO.

The Peace Agreement

The Middle East Peace Conference convened in Madrid, Spain, in 1991. While further meetings were taking place in Washington in 1992, a tiny group of PLO and Israeli delegates met secretly in Norway. Their discussions continued for 15 months. On September 13, 1993, Prime Minister Yitzhak Rabin of Israel and Yasir Arafat, head of the PLO, signed a peace agreement in Washington.

Some of the terms were:

1. The PLO would have jurisdiction over the city of Jericho and the Gaza Strip.

2. The PLO would have jurisdiction over police, fire, health, water, and education.

3. Israel would have jurisdiction over borders, roads, and the protection of Jewish settlements in the PLO enclaves.

4. A phased Israeli troop withdrawal would begin on December 13, 1993. Within nine months Israel would withdraw from all West Bank cities. Soon after that it would transfer all remaining land except the Jewish settlements to the Palestinian National Authority.

5. The final status of the territories would be settled at the end of five years.

On September 3, 1993, the Israeli Knesset, which has 120 members, approved the peace agreement by a vote of 61 to 50. Although all Israelis yearn for peace, many did not trust Arafat and the PLO, and felt that Israel was giving up too much too soon. Victory came, as expected, from the 44 members of Rabin's own party, 12 votes from the leftist Meretz party, and 5 votes from the Israeli Arab Knesset members. Without the Arab votes the agreement would not have been ratified.

Prime Minister Yitzhak Rabin, and Yasir Arafat in Washington. President Bill Clinton negotiated a handshake between these two enemies.

Qalqilya

As part of the agreement, Israel agreed to withdraw the IDF from six major Arab cities in Judea and Samaria: Qalqilya, Ramallah, Jenin, Bethlehem, Tulkarm, and Hebron. Israel has kept its part of the agreement, and has withdrawn from all cities. As part of its agreement, there is a small detachment of Israeli troops to protect the 450 Jews who live in Hebron.

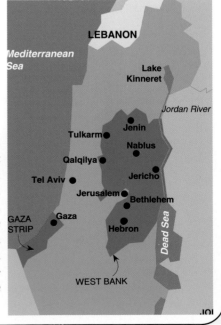

The Oslo accords stipulated that Israeli troops would withdraw from all West Bank cities. Israeli troops have not been withdrawn from Hebron because of the danger from the hostile Arab population.

Reasons for the Agreement

On September 13, 1993, Prime Minister Yitzhak Rabin and Yasir Arafat signed a peace agreement in which Israel and the PLO recognized each other's right to exist.

The negotiations for this historic agreement took place in Norway over a period of 15 months. After so many years of warfare the two combatants decided, each for its own reasons, that it was time to call a halt and seek an accommodation.

The Palestinian Reasons

1. Hamas, the extremist party, was getting stronger and gaining more and more recruits. The influence of the PLO was slowly being eroded. In time its ability to command the loyalty of the Palestinians would disappear. Its prestige would be restored if it gained control of part of the occupied territories.

2. The PLO government in exile was bankrupt. During the Gulf War, the PLO had sided with Iraq against Kuwait and Saudi Arabia. At the end of the war the two kingdoms cut off their financial support for the PLO. As a result, the PLO had not paid its employees and military personnel for many months. Without financial support, it would have to disband its guerilla troops.

3. During the Cold War the Russians had supported the PLO politically in the United Nations. They had also supplied it with weapons and money. Now that the Soviet Union had broken up and the Cold War had ended, Russia lost interest in the Middle East and the PLO.

The Israeli Reasons

The Israelis also had some special reasons for seeking a peaceful, though imperfect, solution to the Palestinian problem.

1. Israel had been at war for 45 years since 1948, and many Israelis were psychologically and physically tired. Three generations of Israelis, grandparents, parents, and children, had tasted the bitterness of war, and a majority of them were ready for some sort of compromise.

2. Hamas, the extreme wing of the Arab liberation movement, was gaining strength. Its terrorists were totally dedicated to the destruction of Israel. The security situation within Israel would worsen if Hamas gained control of the Arab masses.

3. Hundreds of thousands of Russian immigrants had come to Israel. Many of them were highly educated and skilled professionals. Israeli economists believed that peace with the neighboring Arab countries would provide a beneficial dividend. Israel would be transformed into a high-technology center for the entire Middle East and thus be able to provide work for the immigrants.

Israeli and Palestinian policemen on joint patrol.

Hebron Pre-1967

The ancient farming city of Hebron is located 19 miles south of Jerusalem, high atop the Judean Mountains. Situated 3,000 feet above sea level, it is the loftiest of Israel's four holy cities. The presence of the Cave of Machpelah makes it Judaism's second-holiest site, surpassed only by Jerusalem.

Surrounded by a towering wall of huge stones that may have come from Solomon's Temple, the Cave of Machpelah dominates the history of Hebron.

According to the Midrash, the Cave of Machpelah is the burial place of Adam and Eve, who settled in Hebron after they were expelled from the Garden of Eden.

Later on, Abraham, the first Patriarch, purchased the Cave of Machpelah from Ephron the Hittite for 400 silver shekels. There he buried his beloved wife Sarah. Subsequently Isaac and Rebecca, and Jacob and Leah, were also interred there.

As a reminder of the four holy couples buried in the Cave of Machpelah, Hebron is called Kiryat Arba ("City of Four").

Jews revere the Cave of Machpelah as the burial place of the Patriarchs and Matriarchs. Muslims venerate it as Al-Haram Al-Ibrahimi, the tomb of Abraham.

As we know from the Torah, Abraham had two sons, Isaac and Ishmael. The Torah records a prophecy that Ishmael would become "the father of a great nation." Based on this prophecy, the Koran, Islam's sacred book, identifies Ishmael as the ancestor of the Arabs.

Around 3,000 years ago, Hebron was King David's capital before he conquered

The Cave of Machpelah, where the patriarchs are buried, is behind the ancient walls of Hebron.

Jerusalem. The city was destroyed by the Romans in the first century C.E., and the Byzantines built a Christian church on the site of the Cave of Machpelah.

Under Byzantine rule Jews were not permitted to reside in Hebron. The city's Jewish community was reborn after the Arab invasion in the eighth century. Caliph Omar, the Muslim ruler, allowed Hebron's Jewish inhabitants to build a synagogue and a cemetery near the Cave of Machpelah. The Muslim conquerors converted the Christian church at the Cave into a mosque.

From the commercial and religious documents discovered in the Cairo Geniza by Solomon Schechter, it can be seen that there was a substantial Jewish population in Hebron during the Arab period. However, when the crusaders captured the city in 1100, they expelled all the Jews. They turned the mosque and the adjoining synagogue into a church.

When the Muslims regained control,

they built a wall at the entrance of the Cave in which they put a small window through which Jews could pray. The decree prohibiting Jews (and Christians) from entering the holy shrine was strictly enforced by the Arabs and remained in effect until 1967, when Israeli troops captured Hebron during the Six-Day War.

Under Mamluk rule, from 1260 to 1570, Jews were allowed to live in Hebron but were forbidden to enter the Cave of Machpelah. After the Expulsion in 1492, Jews escaping from Spain settled in the city. Under Ottoman Turkish rule they helped to make Hebron a center for the study of Kabbalah.

Teenage students in a Hebron yeshiva. More than 20 of these youngsters were massacred during the 1929 riot.

In 1929, however, the peaceful Jews of Hebron were attacked by a frenzied Arab mob determined to drive them out. In the ensuing riot, during which the British police refused to intervene, 69 Jewish men, women, and children were murdered. Their homes were looted, their businesses were vandalized, and the city's synagogues were burned. The Jewish community of Hebron was totally destroyed.

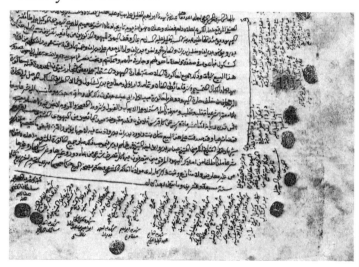

Over the centuries the Jews of Hebron have always legally purchased the land they occupied. In biblical times Abraham purchased the Cave of Machpelah from Ephron the Hittite for 400 silver shekels. In 1807, Chayim Ha-Mitzri purchased 4 dunams of land from an Arab. The illustration is a facsimile of the deed transferring the property.

The Jewish community of Hebron dwindled during World War I but revived after General Allenby's British soldiers captured the city in 1918. Within a few years a prosperous and pious Jewish community had developed.

The Arab rioters in 1929 demolished or burned all of Hebron's synagogues. This Jewish survivor managed to salvage a Torah scroll from the ruins of a synagogue.

Hebron Under Israeli Rule

As a result of the Six-Day War in 1967, Hebron came under Israeli rule as part of the territory of Judea and Samaria. The Israeli government restored the right to worship at Abraham's tomb but did not allow Jews to settle in the city. In 1972, as a compromise, it permitted a group of settlers to establish the community of Kiryat Arba about half a mile from the Cave of Machpelah.

Seven years later, in 1979, Rabbanit Miriam Levinger audaciously led a group of women and children into Hebron, where they reoccupied the old Hadassah Hospital in the old Jewish quarter, which had been destroyed by the Arab rioters in 1929. A eight-month standoff followed, and finally the Israeli government reversed its policy, allowing Jews to live in the hospital building.

By 1994 the Jewish community of Hebron numbered 400. Despite the hardships and the hostility of the city's Arab inhabitants, the Jewish settlers, men, women, and children, lead secure and religiously meaningful lives under the protection of the IDF.

On February 24, 1994, Dr. Baruch Goldstein, a resident of Kiryat Arba, entered the Cave of Machpelah and opened fire on the Muslim worshippers. He killed 29 Arabs and was himself beaten to death. Dr. Goldstein, an American-born oleh, had been a follower of Rabbi Meir Kahane, a Jewish political leader who in 1990 was assassinated by a Muslim in New York City. According to friends and relatives, Dr. Goldstein was deeply troubled by the Rabin-Arafat peace agreement and feared that it threatened Israel's national well-being.

It is obscene to compare massacres. Nothing can justify the murder of a single human being, Arab or Jew, yet some say it is important to identity the differences between the Hebron massacres of 1929 and 1994.

In 1929 hundreds of highly organized Arab rioters attacked a peaceful Jewish community and murdered innocent men, women, and children. The rioters plundered Jewish homes and businesses, and burned synagogues. They did this even though there was no Israeli government or militant Jewish settlers to arouse their anger. The mere presence of a few Jews in Hebron was enough to provoke a massacre. When the riot was over, not even one Arab official bothered to express sympathy or to apologize.

In contrast, the 1994 massacre was the act of one deranged man, on his own, who felt abandoned by his government and was deeply troubled about the many Arab terrorist attacks on Jews that had taken place in the preceding months. In the aftermath, Israel's highest officials, starting with Prime Minister Yitzchak Rabin, apologized publicly for the murders. Moreover, Israel is paying compensation to the families of the victims.

The Assasination of Rabin

Saturday night, November 4, 1995, was one of the most fateful times in the history of modern Israel. On that darkest of nights, Yitzhak Rabin, Israeli's Prime Minister and one of its great military heroes, was assassinated.

That evening 100,000 Israelis had assembled in Tel Aviv to participate in a political rally. Rabin delivered a speech and joined in singing the "Song of Peace." After the rally Rabin and Shimon Peres began to walk to their cars.

Lurking in the dark shadows of the night, a young assassin named Yigal Amir was waiting. As Rabin approached his limousine, Amir quietly stepped out of the shadows and from about a yard away pumped three bullets point blank into the Prime Minister.

Entering the Old City of Jerusalem, *from left to right:* Chief of Staff Gen. Uzi Narkiss, Defense Minister Moshe Dayan, Gen. Yitzhak Rabin, commander of the Central Sector.

Among the foreign dignitaries paying their last respects to Yitzhak Rabin were (*from left to right*) President Bill Clinton, former Presidents Jimmy Carter, and George Bush, Queen Beatrice of the Netherlands, Mrs. Peres and Prime Minister Shimon Peres, Queen Nur and King Hussein of Jordan.

Rabin was rushed to a nearby hospital, where he died on the operating table. The shocked nation went into mourning, and the spot where Rabin was shot became a shrine filled with memorial candles, flowers, and posters.

Rabin's funeral was attended by President Bill Clinton, former Presidents Bush, Carter, and Ford, and the leaders of many other countries, including President Mubarak of Egypt and King Hussein of Jordan. Rabin was succeeded as Prime Minister by Shimon Peres, who vowed to continue his policies.

YITZHAK RABIN (1922–1995) served his country both as a soldier and as a diplomat. Born in Jerusalem, he graduated from the Kadoori agricultural school. In 1940, he enlisted in the Palmach and participated in numerous underground actions against the British Mandate. In 1946, he was arrested by the British and imprisoned for six months. During the War of Independence, Rabin commanded the Harel Brigade, which was active in the battle for Jerusalem. Appointed Chief of Staff in 1964, he led Israel's forces to victory in the Six-Day War of 1967. After serving as Israel's ambassador to the United States, Rabin became Prime Minister in 1974–77 and was reelected in 1992. On November 4, 1995, he was assassinated by Yigal Amir.

The Election of 1999

On June 2, 1996 Benjamin Netanyahu (b. 1949), of the Likud Party, defeated Shimon Peres and became Israel's new Prime Minister. His victory was in large part due to public disquiet about the way the peace agreement with the PLO was proceeding. While Israel had been carrying out all of its commitments, the PLO was not. It had not modified its covenant to eliminate language calling for the destruction of the Jewish state. Even worse, terrorist attacks had become increasingly more frequent and brutal. While Israelis desperately wanted peace, a majority of voters agreed with Netanyahu that it was necessary to proceed cautiously and slowly, and with more concern for security than Peres had shown.

Benjamin Netanyahu

Netanyahu was the first sabra Prime Minister of Israel. Although born in Israel, he lived for several years in the United States and earned degrees in business and architecture from the Massachusetts Institute of Technology. In 1967 he returned to Israel to serve in the army. As an officer in an elite commando unit, he played an important part in the team that rescued hostages from a hijacked Belgian plane in 1972. He served as Israel's United Nations ambassador in the 1980s and was also Deputy Foreign Minister.

The Wye River Accord

Arafat and Netanyahu, on September 28, 1998, cleared the way for summit negotiations during a three-way meeting with President Clinton in Washington. On October 23, 1998 in Washington, D.C. they signed an interim agreement on conditions for an Israeli military withdrawal from parts of the West Bank.

The accord, known as the Wye River Memorandum, would implement the second of three Israeli pullbacks from the West Bank as outlined in the second-phase agreement signed by the two sides in September 1995.

President Clinton intervened in the talks to move them toward completion and Jordan's King Hussein left his sickbed to visit the site, underscoring the urgency of the undertaking. Sadly, several months later King Hussein, a strong advocate for peace, died of cancer.

On November 7, 1998, the PLO executive committee, in accordance with the terms of the Memorandum, confirmed that all articles in the PLO charter calling for the destruction of Israel were null and void.

Highlights Of The Accord

The Wye River accord expanding Palestinian self-rule on the West Bank, was signed by Israeli Prime Minister Netanyahu and President Yasser Arafat, on October 23, 1998 in Washington, D.C. President Clinton signed the document as a witness.

- Under terms of the agreement the Israeli military withdrawal from 13.1 per cent of the West Bank was to be carried out in three stages over three months.
- Upgrading of Palestinian Authority anti-terrorism measures.
- Reduction of the Palestinian Authority police force.
- Arrest of terrorist suspects, and confiscation of illegal weapons.
- Release of 750 Palestinian prisoners held in Israeli jails.
- Opening of a Palestinian airport and industrial park in the Gaza Strip.
- Opening of a transportation corridor to allow Palestinians to travel between the West Bank and the Gaza Strip.

With U.S. President Clinton in attendance, on December 14, 1998 the PA voted to cancel all articles in the 1964 Palestinian Charter that called for the destruction of Israel.

Netanyahu Under Attack

The Wye River accord came under attack from all corners of the Israeli political spectrum. Netanyahu's acceptance of the Wye Memorandum which outlined a further stage of Israeli military withdrawals from the West bank caused the rightist coalition to unravel. Following the Knesset rejection of this peace program the Prime Minister attempted to establish a national unity government. Despite the defections, Netanyahu expressed confidence that he would win re-election, but he lost.

Jerusalem and the Arabs

One of the most important issues in the Arab-Israeli dispute is the control of Jerusalem.

This holy city has always played a central religious and political role in Jewish life. King David recognized its importance and made it the capital of ancient Israel. King Solomon made Jerusalem the religious center of Judaism by erecting the Holy Temple there. According to rabbinic tradition, Jerusalem is the center of God's spiritual world.

During the 2,000 years of exile, Jews never lost their love for the holy city. As they were led into Babylonian captivity in 586 B.C.E., they tearfully sang:

If I forget thee, Jerusalem,
May my right hand lose its cunning,
May my tongue cleave to its palate.

There are many references to Jerusalem in the daily, Sabbath, and holiday prayers. Worshippers in the synagogue always face toward Jerusalem.

In every generation there has been a Jewish presence in Jerusalem. Jews continued to worship at the ancient Western Wall. Because of the tears of exile, the Wall was often called the Wailing Wall.

As part of the 1949 armistice agreement, the United Nations split Jerusalem into two parts, the New City to be controlled by Israel, the Old City and its holy shrines, by Jordan. The agreement stated that Jews would have free access to worship at the Western Wall and the shrines in the Old City.

In spite of the agreement, the Jordanians did not allow Jews to worship at the Western Wall. To further aggravate the situation, they vandalized the Jewish cemetery on the Mount of Olives and destroyed many of the Old City's historic synagogues.

In 1967, during the Six-Day War, Israel captured the Old City and reunited Jerusalem.

Jerusalem is sacred to three religions: Judaism, Christianity, and Islam. The Israeli government guarantees all religions freedom of access to their holy places and shrines. Everyone is free to worship God in complete freedom.

The Muslim View of Jerusalem

The two holiest cities of Islam are Mecca and Medina. Mecca is where Muhammad, the founder of Islam, was born. Medina is where he preached and developed the Muslim religion. Jerusalem is also considered a holy city by Muslims, although its role in the earliest years of Islam was comparatively minor.

Muslims believe that Muhammad, in a dream, was transported up to heaven from the Temple Mount in Jerusalem. In the 7th century, several decades after the Muslim conquest of Jerusalem, Caliph Abd Malik ibn Marwan built the Mosque of Omar on the site where Muhammad's dream was said to have occurred—the exact spot where the First

The Old City of Jerusalem is divided into four sections or quarters: Jewish, Arab, Christian, and Armenian. The Christian quarter contains many churches, schools, and important historical and religious sites.

and Second Temples had stood some 1,600 years earlier.

Jerusalem and the Palestinian Authority

The Palestinians insist that East Jerusalem must be the capital of the state they hope to establish on the West Bank. Israel maintains that Jerusalem is and will always be Israel's capital—to quote Yitzhak Rabin, "Jerusalem is the ancient and eternal capital of the Jewish people."

Because of these seemingly irreconcilable positions, the peace treaty with the PLO refers to Jerusalem in deliberately vague language. Israeli and Arab diplomats hope to solve the questions pertaining to the holy city before the treaty goes into full effect.

Jerusalem and the United States

Despite the bonds of friendship between Israel and the United States, the U.S. government continues to locate its embassy in Tel Aviv. The State Department refuses to recognize Jerusalem as the capital of Israel. In addition, it maintains a separate American consulate in East Jerusalem for the convenience of Palestinians.

The U.S. Senate has passed a resolution which requires the the State

The golden dome of the Mosque of Omar in Jerusalem is a highly visible landmark. It was built by Caliph Abd Malik ibn Marwan in 691 C.E.

Department to move the American embassy to Jerusalem, but no steps in this direction have been taken.

POPULATION MAP OF THE LARGEST CITIES IN ISRAEL

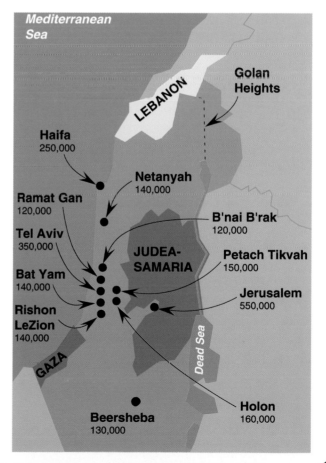

Mediterranean Sea

LEBANON

Golan Heights

Haifa
250,000

Netanyah
140,000

Ramat Gan
120,000

B'nai B'rak
120,000

Tel Aviv
350,000

JUDEA-SAMARIA

Petach Tikvah
150,000

Bat Yam
140,000

Jerusalem
550,000

Rishon LeZion
140,000

GAZA

Dead Sea

Holon
160,000

Beersheba
130,000

The Knesset building in Jerusalem. The Knesset is the legislative body of the State of Israel. Its 120 members are elected by a secret ballot.

Israel and Jordan

When Israel became independent in May 1948, Jordan's Arab Legion joined in the attack on it and occupied East Jerusalem, Judea, and Samaria. Jordan gave citizenship to thousands of Arab refugees from Israel. After the Six-Day War in 1967, Jordan lost control of Jerusalem, Judea, and Samaria to Israel, but its population still included a huge number of Palestinians. In September 1970—known in the PLO's annals as Black September—Yasir Arafat and his guerilla fighters tried to overthrow Hussein's government. Syria planned to invade Jordan at the same time, but was prevented by the threat of Israeli intervention. Thanks to Israel's support, the Arab Legion crushed the Palestinian revolt. The PLO, expelled from Jordan, found a new base of operations in Lebanon.

On October 26, 1994, Prime Minister Yitzhak Rabin and Prime Minister Abdul Salam Majali of Jordan signed a peace agreement. The two countries are cooperating in the development of water resources, transportation, postal service, and telecommunications, and have agreed to alleviate the human problems caused by the Middle East conflict. Israel and Jordan have exchanged ambassadors. King Hussein reacted positively to the election of Prime Minister Benjamin Netanyahu in 1996, in part because of concern that a PLO state on the West Bank would be as much of a danger to Jordan as to Israel.

King Hussein has shown his skill as a survivor on the Arab political map. The King is now mending his fences with the PLO and Yasir Arafat. In September 1996 he made an appearance with Arafat and voiced his support for the political ambitions of the PLO.

King Hussein

March 13, 1997

A Jordanian soldier opened fire and killed seven girls from an orthodox Jewish high school, and wounded eight. In a gesture of consolation, King Hussein visited the bereaved families and offered his heart-felt apologies and condolences.

Signing the peace treaty between Israel and Jordan. President Clinton (*front row, center*) and Secretary of State Warren Christopher (*rear row, second from left*) participated in and signed the agreement.

Ehud Barak

Ehud was the heroic biblical judge who defeated the Moabites and ended several generations of rule over Israel. Barak (which means "lightning" in Hebrew) was the bold military commander who joined forces with the prophetess Deborah and defeated the Canaanites under Sisera. Two very descriptive names for Israel's most decorated soldier.

On May 18, 1999 Ehud Barak was elected Prime Minister of Israel.

Barak is the child of Zionist pioneers who fled from Lithuania after Cossacks murdered their parents. He was born on February 12, 1942 on a kibbutz in the Heffer Valley near the Lebanese border. Ehud spent a 36-year career in the Israel defense forces, and served as a platoon leader, a tank battalion commander, an intelligence analyst and and from 1991 to 1995 he was chief of the Israeli Army General Staff. Barak is the most decorated soldier in Israel's history.

Lt. General Ehud Barak left the military in 1995 and was appointed Interior Minister in Yitzhak Rabin's government. After the assassination of Rabin in 1995, Shimon Peres appointed him to the post of Foreign Minister. In 1997, after Netanyahu defeated Shimon Peres, he became the leader of the Labor Party.

In addition to his military career, Ehud Barak's credentials includes a degree in physics and mathematics from the Hebrew University in Jerusalem. He also has a Master's Degree from Stanford University, in economic engineering systems.

A Commitment To Peace

During the 1999 election campaign, Barak stressed his commitment to the peace process. In 1994 as Army Chief of Staff under Prime Minister Rabin he supervised the first troop withdrawals from Jericho and Gaza, and played an important role in securing a peace treaty with Jordan.

Barak defeated Netanyahu 56% to 44% The Palestinians helped by controlling the terrorists and blurring security issues which would have helped Netanyahu. Barak's march to victory also came from a shift to labor by many thousands of Russians who emigrated to Israel.

A Time Of Transition

In his first two weeks as Prime Minister, Barak re-energized an exhausted peace process. Israel's most decorated soldier met Arab leaders and moved to carry out the stalled land-for-peace deal with Palestinian Authority President Yasir Arafat. Barak also embarked on an ambitious agenda: to make peace not only with the Palestinians but also with Syria and Lebanon. His idea is to set in place a series of treaties which would end all the wars between Israel and its Arab neighbors.

Clearly, Barak means business. It will take political skill to achieve the goals he has set for himself. His view of peace with the Palestinians, is tough and unromantic. Barak visualizes "a physical separation" from the Arabs. He has also vowed never to give up

Israeli sovereignty over any part of Jerusalem, which Palestinians also claim as their capital.

Talks with Syria are going nowhere, and Assad who is in failing health refuses to discuss normalizing relations with the Jewish state.

The Agreement

On September 5, 1999 in Sharm El-Sheikh, Prime Minister Barak of Israel and Yasir Arafat, the Palestinian leader signed a broad peace agreement. The ceremony was attended by President Hosni Mubarak of Egypt, King Abdullah II of Jordan and Madeleine Albright, the American Secretary of State. The agreement represented a step which everyone hopes will usher in a new era of peace across the region.

Starting on September 13, 1999 the Israelis will, in three stages, transfer control of 40% of the West Bank to the Palestinians. As of September 8, 1999 the first pullback by Israeli forces had taken place.

On October 1, 1999 Israel will open a passage connecting Gaza with the West Bank. Also, on October 1st construction will begin on a seaport in Gaza. Israel has also agreed to release 350 Arab prisoners.

The Palestinians have agreed to collect illegal weapons and to submit a list of security officers and to accept a date for the "final status" negotiations.

Barak has set his timetable and envisions a regional peace in 15 months. Arafat, 70 and in precarious health, wants to deliver to his people a Palestinian state within the pre-established time.

A New Terrorist Attack

Less than 24 hours after the new Israeli Palestinian Peace Accord was signed, two cars parked with explosives blew up in two Israeli cities. In Haifa and Tiberias the Arab occupants of the two cars blew themselves up. Several Israeli passers-by were wounded. Security officers have evidence that both sets of bombers were members of Hamas and Islamic Holy War factions.

The latest agreement obligates Israel to release prisoners who have committed terrorist acts against the state. The two terror attacks within 24 hours after the agreement has called that policy into question.

At the signing ceremony in Egypt were, from left, King Abdullah II of Jordan, Ehud Barak of Israel, Hosni Mubarak of Egypt, Yasir Arafat, the Palestinian leader, and Secretary of State Madelaine K. Albright.

Israel and the Jews of Russia

Since the beginning, the lives of Russian Jews have been difficult and permeated with anti-Semitism. Each of the governing regimes, from the tsars to the Communists, have imposed restrictions on economic opportunities and on Jewish cultural and religious expression.

Leon Trotsky (Lev Davidovich, 1879–1940) was exiled to Siberia in 1898 for revolutionary activities, but in 1902 he escaped to England. During the October Revolution in 1917 he returned and played an important part in the Communist uprising. Leon Trotsky organized the Red Army. In 1929 he was exiled by Stalin and went to Mexico, where he was murdered by the Russian secret police. To the very end he was antagonistic to Judaism. Leon Trotsky, seated in the center, is shown with a group of army officers, some of whom were Jews.

During the black years of the Stalin era, from 1919 to 1953, Soviet Jewry was decimated, first by the Nazis and then by the Communist regime. Over half of Russia's enormous Jewish community, which at one time totaled over 5 million, was murdered in the Holocaust. At the end of

Joseph Stalin (1879–1953) ruthlessly eliminated all of his political rivals after the death of Lenin. The police state he created murdered more than 20 million Russians.

World War II, Stalin launched a campaign to destroy Jewish cultural and religious identity. Tens of thousands of Jewish intellectuals and professionals were murdered, and hundreds of thousands were exiled to Siberia in a wave of terror.

Stalin's death brought some relief, but official anti-Semitism still limited Jewish economic, cultural, and religious life. The establishment of the State of Israel in 1948, awakened a spirit of hope and the struggle for the right to immigrate. Jewish refuseniks led by Anatole Sharansky challenged the regime by organizing hunger strikes and secret groups for the teaching of Judaism.

Golda Meir, Israel's first ambassador to the USSR, mobbed by Moscow Jews outside the synagogue, Rosh Hashanah, 1948.

By the end of the 1970s, the USSR was in an economic crisis and the political infrastructure was in a state of collapse. When Mikhail Gorbachev became Premier, in 1985, he set in motion the policy of perestroika (reorganization) and removed all emigration barriers. Gorbachev's policy of glasnost (openness) officially permitted cultural, religious, and political activities and unloosened a flood of Jewish emigration to Israel, America, and other countries.

Boris Yeltsin

The reelection in 1995 of President Boris Yeltsin was much better than a loss could have been. Yeltsin's opponents conducted a campaign filled with smears and open anti-Semitism and a loss could have had a catastrophic affect on Russian Jewry. As of 1997, Jews, despite the bureaucracy, were free to emigrate to Israel and anywhere else they pleased.

Internally, the Russian Jewish community is making progress. Individual groups are pooling their resources under an umbrella organization called the Russian Jewish Congress. Their aim is threefold: fund-raising, fighting anti-Semitism and Jewish education.

Russian and Israeli authorities have established transit schools called Ma'ariv schools to facilitate those intending to make aliyah. These schools, much like an American day school, provide a secular program as well as a Hebrew language and Judaic studies curriculum.

Jewish culture and religion are being introduced and spread by Orthodox, Lubavitch, Conservative, Reconstructionist, and Reform groups. They have organized a rainbow of synagogues and managed to attract thousands of worshippers.

Jewish sports clubs—a part of the Maccabee movement—attract 50,000 youngsters with a variety of programs. In addition to sports, the youngsters are exposed to Jewish music, culture, and religious activities.

For more than 70 years Russia was a Jewish cultural desert. Now, through the committed efforts of world Jewry, the Russian Jewish community, which some believe numbers about 1.5 million, is slowly making progress and struggling to regain its former stature.

Boris Yeltsin

The United Jewish Appeal has established a youth program called Naaleh, ("we will go up"). It sends thousands of Jewish teenagers from Russia to Israel, to complete high school and prepare for college. This experience has encouraged many of them to settle in Israel.

The Joint Distribution Committee has throughout the years shipped matzot to Russia for Passover. With the help of the JDC, local committees in the former Soviet Union are producing their own. This matzah factory in Kiev provides for the needs of Jews in Ukraine, Belarus, and Moldova.

Time Chart

B.C.E.

ca. 2000–1750	Age of the patriarchs and matriarchs
ca. 1750–1400	Israel in Egypt
ca. 1400–1250	Moses, exodus from Egypt
ca. 1250–1050	Conquest of Canaan; period of the judges
ca. 1030–1006	Saul, first king of Israel
ca. 1006–965	David rules Israel; Jerusalem becomes capital of Israel
ca. 965–930	Solomon succeeds David; First Temple built
ca. 925	United kingdom split into Israel and Judea
721	Assyria conquers Israel
586	Babylonia conquers Judea; Jews exiled to Babylon.
538	First return, led by Sheshbazzar
520–515	Temple rebuilt under Persian rule
ca. 458	Persian Emperor Artaxerxes allows Jews to return; Nehemiah rebuilds walls of Jerusalem; Ezra reads Torah
336–323	Alexander the Great defeats Persians and conquers Israel
ca. 223–184	Antiochus III conquers Israel
ca. 175–165	Maccabean revolt against Antiochus IV
ca. 165	Judah Maccabee rededicates Temple; feast of Hanukkah
ca. 141	Judea an independent state
ca. 63	Romans occupy Palestine

ca. 37–4	Herod rules Judea
ca. 19	Herod rebuilds Temple

C.E.

30	Jesus crucified by Romans
66–70	First Revolt against Rome
70	Fall of Jerusalem; Sanhedrin reestablished
73	Masada falls to Romans
132–135	Second Revolt, led by Bar Kochba; Betar falls
313–635	Byzantine rule
425	Jerusalem Talmud compiled
500	Babylonian Talmud completed
614–629	Jewish rule in Jerusalem under Persians
622–632	Islam founded by Muhammad
638	Jerusalem conquered by Arabs
1078	Jerusalem conquered by Seljuk Turks
1092–1096	First Crusade
1492	Jews expelled from Spain; some settle in Israel
1517–1917	Ottoman Turks rule Israel
1882–1904	Pogroms in Russia; First Aliyah
1858–1922	Eliezer Ben-Yehuda, father of modern Hebrew
1860–1904	Theodor Herzl; Dreyfus Affair
1894	First Zionist Conference in Basle
1904–1914	Second Aliyah from Russia and Poland
1917	Balfour Declaration
1919–1948	British rule Palestine
1873–1934	Hayim Nahman Bialik, Is-

Time Chart

	rael's most famous poet
1880–1978	Shmuel Yosef Agnon, Nobel Prize for Literature
1919–1923	Third Aliyah from Poland
1924–28	Fourth Aliyah
1933	Hitler; rise of Nazism; Fifth Aliyah from Germany
1939	British White Paper
1939–1945	World War II; Holocaust
1947	United Nations resolution dividing Palestine between Jews and Arabs; discovery of Dead Sea Scrolls
1948	State of Israel established; War of Independence
1949	Israel admitted to United Nations
1948–1952	Mass immigration from Arab countries and Europe
1956	Sinai Campaign
1962	Adolph Eichmann executed
1967	Six-Day War; Jerusalem united
1973	Yom Kippur War
1977	Anwar Sadat addresses Knesset; Likud comes to power
1978	Camp David peace agreement
1979	Israel-Egypt peace treaty signed
1981	Israel destroys Iraqi nuclear reactor
1982	Israel withdraws from Sinai; Operation Peace for Galilee
1984	National Unity govern-

	ment formed
1987	Palestine uprising (intifada) begins
1989	Peace initiative proposed by Israel; mass immigration of Soviet Jews begins
1991	Iraq attacks Kuwait; Saddam Hussein attacks Israel with Scud missiles during Gulf War; Middle East Peace Conference convenes
1992	Israeli establishes diplomatic relations with China
1993	Israel and PLO sign a peace agreement. Israel and Vatican establish full diplomatic relations. United Nations endorses Israel-PLO peace treaty.
1994	Israel and the PLO sign a Peace Accord, granting self-rule to the Gaza Strip and Jericho. President Assad of Syria indicates desire for peace with Israel.

Glossary

ALUF — Hebrew title of Israeli general.

ASHKENAZI — Jew of central or eastern Europe ancestry.

AV — Eleventh month of Hebrew calendar.

BAGRUT — Tests which Israeli students must pass before being admitted to a university.

ERETZ YISRAEL — State of Israel.

ETROG — Citron used on Sukkot.

GEMARA — Aramaic summary of legal debates on meaning of Mishnah.

GENIZAH — Room or depository where torn and discarded holy books and religious objects are stored.

HAGANAH — Secret Jewish military group in Palestine during British Mandate.

HALUTZ — Jewish pioneer in Palestine before the independence of Israel.

HANUKKAH — Festival of Lights.

HAREDIM — Ultra-Orthodox Jews.

HASHOMER — Jewish watchmen who protected Yishuv against Arab thieves and raiders during early 1900's.

HASID (pl. HASIDIM) — Member of Orthodox religious sect founded by Baal Shem Tov.

HAVER (pl. HAVERIM) — Lit. "Friend"; member of Knesset.

HOLOCAUST — Murder of six million Jews by Nazis.

IDF — Israel Defense Forces.

IYAR — Eighth month of Hebrew calendar.

KABBALAH — Jewish mysticism

KIBBUTZ — Agricultural settlement with shared community property.

KNESSET — The parliament of Israel.

KOL YISRAEL — Israeli radio and television network.

LULAV — Palm branch used on Sukkot.

MAABARAH — Temporary camp for Israeli immigrants.

MALKOT — Israeli paddleball game.

MAMLUKS — Muslim soldiers of Christian origin.

MANDATE — Period of British rule over Palestine after World War I.

MINYAN — Quorum of ten Jews needed for public prayer.

Glossary

MISHNAH   Six-part legal code, developed in Palestine during first and second centuries.

MOSHAV   Cooperative settlement.

MOSSAD   Israeli security service operating outside Israel.

NASI   1. President of Sanhedrin during the talmudic period; 2. Title of President of Israel.

NEGEV   Southern desert region of Israel.

OLIM   Immigrants who settle in Israel.

OMER   Measure of barley donated to Temple during 49 days between Passover and Shavuot.

ROSH HASHANAH
  Jewish New Year.

SABRA   Person born in Israel.

SEDER   Passover meal at which the story of Israelite Exodus from Egypt is re-enacted.

SEPHARDI   Descendent of Spanish or Portuguese Jews.

SHAVUOT   Lit, "Weeks"; festival celebrated seven weeks after Passover.

SHOFAR   Ram's horn blown in synagogue on Rosh Hashanah and Yom Kippur.

SHULCHAN ARUCH
  Code of Jewish law.

TALMUD   Massive legal work combining Mishnah and Gemara.

TEL   Archaelogical site.

TISHA B'AV   Ninth day of the month of Av; day of fasting and mourning.

TORAH   Five Books of Moses.

TZAHAL   Israeli army.

YISHUV   Lit. "settlement"; Jewish community in Palestine before Israel became independent.

YOM KIPPUR   Day of Attonement.

Index

PHOTO CREDITS

While every effort has been made to trace and acknowledge all copyright holders, we would like to apologize for any omissions.

———

Lavon Institute for Labor Research; Yad VaShem; Bibliothèque Nationale, Paris; Jewish National Fund; Government Press Office; Haganah Historical Archives; IDF Archives; Institute of Archeology; Tel Aviv University; Eretz Yisrael Museum; Rockefeller Museum Library; Museum of History of Jerusalem; Israel Postal Authority; Central Zionist Archives; Israel Museum, Jerusalem. David Blatt: 15, Western Wall; 17, Shalom Tower, Mann Auditorium; 18, Haifa Bay; 19, Haifa; 20, Bedouin market; 21, Ben Gurion University; 36, Mashbir; 37, Beilenson Kupat Cholim, Egged; 41, Hasidim at Western Wall; 57, Baling cotton, Kibbutz house; 66, Shrine of the Book; 68, Hechal Shlomo, Hadassah Medical Center, Tiferet Israel; 79, Masada Synagogue, Masada storage rooms; 83, Via Dolorosa; 89, Belvoir Castle; 111, Yad Vashem; 131, Orthodox Jews.